Murder on the White Sands

The Disappearance of
Albert and Henry Fountain

Corey Recko

Number 5 in the A. C. Greene Series

University of North Texas Press
Denton, Texas

10 9 8 7 6 5 4 3 2 1

Permissions:
University of North Texas Press
P.O. Box 311336
Denton, TX 76203-1336

The paper used in this book meets the minimum requirements
of the American National Standard for Permanence of Paper for
Printed Library Materials, z39.48.1984. Binding materials have
been chosen for durability.

Library of Congress Cataloging-in-Publication Data
Recko, Corey, 1974-
  Murder on the White Sands : the disappearance of Albert and
Henry Fountain / Corey Recko.
     p. cm. -- (A. C. Greene series ; no. 5)
  Includes bibliographical references and index.
  ISBN-13: 978-1-57441-224-6 (cloth : alk. paper)
  ISBN-10: 1-57441-224-8 (cloth : alk. paper)
  1. Murder--New Mexico. 2. Murder--Investigation--New
Mexico. 3. Murder victims--New Mexico. 4. Fountain, Albert
Jennings, 1838-1896. 5. Fountain, Henry, d. 1896. I. Title.
  HV6533.N4R43 2007
  364.152'30922--dc22

                                        2006038400

Murder on the White Sands: The Disappearance of Albert and Henry Fountain is Number 5 in the A. C. Greene Series

To Meg
Thank you for putting up with me during the creation of this book. I know it wasn't easy.

Contents

Illustrations and Maps

Acknowledgments

In addition to the sources listed, I would like to thank the following for their help in making this book possible: Melissa Salazar (New Mexico State Records Center and Archives); Ed Smith and DeAnn Kessler (Lincoln State Monument); Claudia A. Rivers and the staff of the C. L. Sonnichsen Special Collections Department at the University of Texas at El Paso; Yvonne Brooks (Library of Congress); Rose Marie Espinosa, Maura Kenny, Dennis Daily, and the staff at the Rio Grande Historical Collections at New Mexico State University; Donald Burge, Ann M. Massmann, and the staff at University of New Mexico; Pinkerton Inc.; Lori Grumet (Thomas Branigan Memorial Library); Charles E. Nodler Jr. (Missouri Southern State College—George A. Spiva Library); Diane Blode (Palace of the Governors Photo Archives); Sandi Keeton (University of New Mexico Press) for permission to reprint the McNew photo; Chuck Carrig for escorting me to Wildy Well and everyone else at Fort Bliss who made it possible; Jim Eckles (Public Affairs Office, White Sands Missile Range); Charles W. Wood (Oliver Lee Memorial State Park); Frank Perez and The Bowlins-Ft. Sumner Museum; William F. Garrett (Garrett family); Irva Neff (Fraser family); Alvy Ray Smith (Gililland family); Emilie Garcia (Espalin family); Frank Brito (Van Patten family); Jerry W. Wilson; Jack Van Patten; Mary F. Bird and Mary V. Alexander (Gadsden Museum/Fountain family); Leon Metz; Gordon R. Owen. Thank you Linda Wimberly for the fine work on the map. Thank you to my mother and father for your help and support. A very special thanks to all those who read over the manuscript in its various forms and provided me feedback and much needed editing: Don C. Marler, William Carroll, Ron Chrisman, Frederick Nolan, Leon Metz, Gordon Owen, Patrick Burke, Chuck Parsons, and Karen DeVinney (managing editor at UNT Press). Thank you to everyone I've mentioned and anyone I may have missed.

Introduction

It was the end of January 1896 when the Grand Jury adjourned in the town of Lincoln, Territory of New Mexico. Colonel Albert Jennings Fountain had just worked to bring indictments against several men in order to combat the cattle rustling that ran rampant in New Mexico.

His work finished, Fountain, with his eight-year-old son Henry who was along for the trip, left Lincoln on the thirtieth day of January. The pair headed southwest, towards their Mesilla home. The journey, some 150 miles, would take three days. It was a journey that the father and son would not complete, for on the third day they disappeared near the White Sands, an area known for mysterious disappearances. What became of them remains one of New Mexico's greatest mysteries.

The disappearance of the prominent Colonel Fountain and his young son caused outrage throughout the territory. The sheriff, whose deputies were quickly becoming suspects, did little to solve this mystery. His standing was shaky anyway, as his right to the office was being contested in the courts due to charges of fraud in the previous election. The governor, anxious to get action in the Fountain case, sought outside help.

First he called on Pat Garrett, the man who fifteen years earlier had killed Billy the Kid. Then he brought in the Pinkerton National Detective Agency, who sent operative John Fraser. What Garrett and Fraser found was a lawless land torn apart by a political feud, a place where theft and murder often went unpunished. What followed was an investigation that put the lives of every participant in danger.

Along with Pat Garrett, some of New Mexico's most famous citizens were involved in the investigation and subsequent trial.

The list includes Albert Fall, Oliver Lee, Thomas Branigan, Miguel Otero, and Thomas B. Catron.

Albert Fountain, who was equally loved and hated wherever he went, had been a reporter, Indian fighter in the United States Army, lawyer, and newspaper editor, as well as having served in the Texas Senate and New Mexico legislature, the former of which he was majority leader and the latter of which he was speaker. A civic and political leader, Colonel Fountain made as many enemies as friends. More than one attempt was made on his life.

The Territory of New Mexico did not become a state until 1912. A number of reasons contributed to the delay of New Mexico's acceptance into the Union, though the primary reason was the widespread lawlessness. Of all the murders in New Mexico in the years preceding statehood, none did more to damage the territory's standing than the murder of the Colonel Albert J. Fountain and his eight-year-old son Henry.

one

Albert Jennings Fountain

Born Albert Jennings on Staten Island, New York, on October 23, 1838, Albert was the son of Solomon and Catherine Jennings. The name Fountain came from his mother, who descended from a French Huguenot family named de la Fontaine, which later turned into Fountain.[1] Why Albert took the last name Fountain is unknown. One theory is that a mysterious murder in the Jennings family caused many members to take other names.[2] Another suggests that Albert took the Fountain name so as not to give himself away as he searched in China for his then missing father.[3]

Fountain was educated in New York public schools and at Columbia College. It was said that during his Columbia days, at age fifteen, he and five other students went on a tour of Europe and the Far East. It was during this stage of Albert's life that his father, a sea captain, was purportedly lost at sea. In Solomon Jennings's last letter to his wife, written somewhere in the Orient, he wrote that food was running out and his crew was getting restless. He was never heard from again.

In the latter half of the 1850s, Fountain arrived in northern California.[4] He worked various jobs until his introduction to journalism, when he took a job as a reporter for the *Sacramento Union*. On one of his first assignments, he was sent to Nicaragua to cover the William Walker expedition. When Fountain sent back reports that Walker planned to establish a slave-holding republic in Nicaragua, with Walker as president, Fountain was arrested and sentenced to execution by firing squad. The resourceful Fountain, disguised as a woman, slipped aboard a steamship to escape.[5] It would not be the last time he would face death.

He spent the next two years as a clerk in a law office and passed the California State Bar. Then civil war broke out and before the young man could be certified he enlisted in the Union army.[6] On August 26, 1861, Fountain enlisted in Company E, First California Infantry Volunteers. His service record describes him at five-foot seven and one-half inches tall, with brown hair, blue eyes, and a light complexion.[7]

Fountain's company trained in Camp Downey near Oakland. As Fountain quickly moved up in the ranks, his company moved to southern California and then marched east. They never met Confederate forces while in Arizona and New Mexico but did battle the native Apaches.[8]

While stationed in New Mexico, Fountain, now a sergeant, met teenaged Mariana Pérez, who on October 27, 1862, would become his wife.[9] Albert and Mariana's first son Albert had just been born when Fountain, then a lieutenant, was discharged in 1864.[10] Family was very important to the couple. In all, they would have ten children: Albert, Marianita, Edward (killed in 1891), Maggie, Thomas, Jack, Fannie, Henry (died in infancy), Catarina, and finally little Henry.[11]

Amidst Indian raids in New Mexico, Fountain re-enlisted. He nearly lost his life while pursuing some uprising Navajos who had left the Bosque Reservation. He and another man, Corporal Val Sánchez, located the renegade Indians, but before they could return to Fort McRae to notify the colonel of the Indians' location, the fugitives became aware of the pair's presence. The two eventually split up and Fountain was alone when cornered in a narrow pass. His horse was killed and he was shot multiple times, with a bullet left in his thigh, an arrow in his forearm, and another arrow in his shoulder.[12] Fountain described the last attacker who tried to get at him through the pass as "a villainous-looking fellow whose only garment was a red shirt."[13] Fountain shot him dead as he charged. He spent the night alone, trapped under his dead horse.

Sánchez, meanwhile, had arrived at Fort McRae and Fountain was rescued early the next day. He was taken first to McRae and then to Fort Bliss, where he had the arrow removed.[14] During Fountain's recovery, he was seen frequently in the streets of El Paso and became acquainted with the town. When healthy, he moved his wife and now two children to El Paso, where he started a law practice. He became a civic leader, joined the Free Masons (Aztec Lodge No. 130), was appointed and served as customs inspector and chief assistant to the collector of customs, was elected county surveyor, and became a leading organizer of the Republican Party in western Texas.[15]

With the Civil War over and the Reconstruction of the South underway, President Lincoln pushed a reconstruction plan criticized by some as too soft. Following Lincoln's assassination neither his decree nor Congress's rival and far tougher Wade Davis Act was implemented as the fight over what to do with the South continued. The "radical" Republicans wanted the Confederate States to be treated the same as were conquered provinces. Andrew Johnson, the new president, adopted a plan that many thought favored the Southern planter elite, permitting them to pass "black codes" that sought to restrict the rights of freed people and restore land to former owners. As a result, Congress passed the Fourteenth Amendment, stating that persons born in the U.S., regardless of color, were U.S. citizens, and restricting a state's power to limit their rights. Congress also passed a series of Reconstruction Acts that limited state powers and set the terms of rebuilding.[16] Fountain, now a leading Texas Republican, supported the Radical Reconstruction, or "hard-peace."

In the elections of 1869, the Radical Republicans in Texas swept all state offices from the "soft-reconstructionists," including the election of new Governor Edmund J. Davis and of Albert Fountain to the state senate.[17] Fountain served in the Texas Senate for one four-year term. His time in the senate saw Texas readmitted into the Union in 1870. As a senator, Fountain served as majority leader and spearheaded the Frontier Protection Bill, which reactivated the Texas Rangers. During this time, he was a founder of St. Clement's Church.[18]

The senator had another brush with death, this time as the result of a political feud. A man named Frank Williams had become upset with Fountain and Judge Gaylord Clarke. Williams was angry when Fountain failed to find him a patronage job after he had supported him. During a subsequent trial, Clarke issued a "severe and emphatic reprimand" to Williams when his conduct as an attorney in Clarke's court became "abusive and disrespectful."[19] Because Williams was now openly hostile towards the two, Fountain attempted to avoid him.

During a verbal attack on Fountain in Dowell's Saloon, Williams drew his gun on the unarmed Fountain, who had only a cane to defend himself. There is disagreement as to whether Fountain attacked Williams with his cane first, or Williams shot first. Either way, what is known is that Fountain was shot three times. One bullet struck him in the arm, another hit his scalp and sent blood running down his face, and a third penetrated his coat and five letters before striking his pocket watch. Williams retreated after emptying his gun. Fountain, Clarke, and a posse of three men went after him. When the five men found him, Williams shot and killed Clarke at point-blank range, which was followed by a shot from Fountain, who, fifty yards away, fired a bullet that hit Williams in the chest. Williams spun around and hit the ground. As Williams reached for his pistol, another man in the posse shot him in the head.[20]

In 1873, the Fountains, now with five children, returned to settle in Mariana's former home of Mesilla, on the outskirts of Las Cruces. Fountain quickly established a law practice there.[21] Still loyal to the Free Masons, he joined Aztec Lodge No. 3 of Las Cruces. The members included Numa Reymond, who would be involved in a fight to become the Doña Ana County sheriff when Fountain disappeared, and prominent New Mexicans William L. Rynerson and James J. Dolan. William H. H. Llewellyn, who would go on to become a good friend of Fountain, joined the lodge in 1883. Fountain became a leading member of the lodge, serving such posts as deputy grand master, senior grand warden, master, senior warden, and senior deacon.[22]

In 1874, Fountain organized the Mesilla Dramatic Association and designed and painted sets, rewrote plays, and acted. He also founded the newspaper *Mesilla Valley Independent*, publishing its first issue on June 23, 1877. He was chief editor and translated for the weekly Spanish edition, *El Independiente del Valle de la Mesilla*.[23]

It was in 1881 that Fountain, as a court-appointed defense attorney, defended his most famous client, William H. Bonney, also known as Billy the Kid. Though Bonney was found guilty of the murder of Sheriff William Brady, he wrote positively about Albert Fountain. "Mr. A. J. Fountain was appointed to defend me and has done the best he could for me. He is willing to carry the case further if I can raise the money to bear his expense."[24] Bonney was brought to the town of Lincoln and held on the second floor of the courthouse to await his execution. He killed two deputies and escaped. He was eventually tracked down and killed by Pat Garrett on July 14, 1881.

Fountain continued his successful law practice and, as a result, he was appointed an assistant United States district attorney.[25] As captain of the Mesilla Scouts, he led the militia that defended the town from Indian raids. His service in protecting the settlers would move him up further in the ranks, and in 1883 Fountain reached the rank of colonel. His work with the militia brought him into close contact with the area's Indian population, many of whom he went on to befriend.[26]

Fountain also became involved in New Mexico politics. A Republican himself, he took on a group of Republicans known as the "Santa Fe Ring." The ring concentrated on amassing wealth and landholding for its members through control over federal patronage and favors from the territorial government. The head of the Santa Fe Ring was undoubtedly Thomas B. Catron. Its members included such notables as William L. Rynerson, James Dolan, and even lifelong Democrat Lawrence G. Murphy. During and after the Lincoln County War, in which Murphy and Dolan led one side and had close ties to Rynerson, Fountain left the Republican Party, helped form, and was elected president of a party he called the Law and Order Party. At this time, he also relinquished control of the *Mesilla Valley Independent.* Soon after, however, Fountain returned to the Republican Party and worked to fix its problems from the inside.[27]

Albert Jennings Fountain in Militia Uniform (Date and photographer unknown. Courtesy Palace of the Governors [MNM/DCA], Negative No. 9873)

Mesilla. The Plaza, circa 1880
(Courtesy New Mexico State University Library, Archives and Special
Collections, Joe Lopez Family Photographs, RG84-159)

Major Fountain's
Militia in 1883.
Standing (L-R):
Lt. Pedro Pedragon,
Lt. Albert Fountain,
Lt. Maclovio Botello;
Seated: Capt. Eugene
Van Patten, Maj.
Albert J. Fountain,
Capt. Francisco
Salazar.
(Date and photog-
rapher unknown.
Courtesy Palace
of the Governors
[MNM/DCA],
Negative No. 13148)

From inside cover of one
of Albert Fall's law books.
(Author's collection)

two

Enter Albert B. Fall and Other Men of Note

In November 1888, Fountain ran against Democratic newcomer Albert B. Fall for a seat in the New Mexico State Legislature.[1] Fountain won the election and went on to be chosen speaker of the house. While in the legislature, Fountain pushed for public education for both boys and girls, an unpopular idea at the time. He successfully fought to have the state's land grant college situated in Las Cruces. (It now is New Mexico State University.) He also worked vigorously for statehood.[2] The rest of Fountain's life would be intertwined with that of his opponent in the 1888 election. The two men, Fountain as a leader of the Republicans and Fall a soon-to-be leader of the Democrats, grew to despise each other.

Albert Bacon Fall was born in Frankfort, Franklin County, Kentucky, on November 26, 1861.[3] He married Emma Morgan on May 8, 1883, and they settled in New Mexico in 1887.[4] According to his service record, Fall stood five feet, ten and one-half inches tall, had a fair complexion, brown eyes, and black hair.[5] Despite his limited formal education, the former miner rose quickly in the Democratic Party, founded the Las Cruces newspaper *Independent Democrat*, and established a successful law practice. He made it his goal to turn this traditionally Republican state into a Democratic state, with two Democratic senators once statehood was achieved, going so far as to fight to delay statehood until New Mexico was Democratic.[6] Fall was once described as a "cowboy, miner, lawyer, judge, gunfighter, able editor, rough rider, farmer, cavalier, and brevet captain of industry,"[7] which speaks to the life he had ahead of him.

In 1890, Fountain again ran against Fall for a legislative seat. This time Fall won by forty-five votes.[8] The rivalry between the two men only increased. The 1892 elections showed just how far the distrust ran between these two men and the two parties. The Republicans sent in the militia, led by Major William H. H. Llewellyn with Captain Thomas Branigan second in command, to guard the polls. Fall, who argued that the militia was brought in to intimidate voters, countered this move by calling on his friend Oliver Lee to lead some armed men, including James Gililland and William McNew, into town. The Democrats swept the election and Fall went back to the legislature.[9]

Two of the men who came out in the militia would go on to play important roles in trying to solve the murder of Colonel Fountain. William Henry Harrison Llewellyn was born on September 9, 1851, in Monroe, Green County, Wisconsin. Llewellyn attended public schools and then Tabor College. He moved to Montana to mine gold at Trinity Gulch, where he spent eight years, but did not find his fortune. He moved to Nebraska and worked a few jobs before being appointed a special agent in the Justice Department by President Hayes. Llewellyn relocated to New Mexico Territory in 1881, arriving on June 16 at the Mescalero Apache Reservation where he had been appointed Indian agent. Working to improve the conditions of the reservation, he won the respect of the Mescaleros, who referred to him as "Tata Crooked Nose." He moved to Las Cruces in 1885 and began to practice law. Later he served as district attorney of Doña Ana County. Llewellyn was a large man, standing over six feet tall and weighing considerably over two hundred pounds.[10]

Captain Thomas Branigan was born in Edinburgh, Scotland, in 1847. His family came to the United States in 1849 and settled in

Ohio. At only fourteen years of age, Branigan enlisted in the Union Army. After the Civil War, Branigan attended the Mennonite College in Wadsworth, Ohio, before going West in 1867. He served as captain of Indian Police and was involved in the campaign to capture Geronimo. Branigan finally settled in Las Cruces, purchased land, and began the raising of bees for the production of honey. He was also interested in gold mining in Sierra country.[11]

On the other side during the election were Lee, Gililland, and McNew, whom Fall, after his appointment as a district judge in 1893, appointed U. S. Deputy Marshals.[12]

The year 1894 marked the formation of the Southeastern New Mexico Stock Growers' Association. The association was a group of cattle companies and ranchmen whose purpose was to stop the rampant cattle rustling that was hurting their businesses. One of its members was Oliver Lee. Albert Fountain, who drafted the association's constitution and bylaws, was their special investigator and lawyer.[13]

Fountain lobbied for various pieces of legislation and went after cattle rustlers. He had two investigators working for him: Ben Williams, a constable from Las Cruces, and Les Dow, who was a U. S. Marshal from Texas.[14]

Williams and Dow locked on a cattle rustling gang headed by Ely "Slick" Miller, alias Jim Rose, which included Lee Williams, Abram Miller, Doc Evans, and Ed Brown. Located near Socorro, they were suspected of plundering association calf crops to build their own herds and of stealing cattle and horses and driving them to markets in Mexico and Indian Territory. The evidence led to warrants for the arrest of Miller and members of the gang.[15] The trial, which began in late November, took place in Roswell because of a change of venue to Chaves County. Ed Brown was missing, but proceedings continued against the rest of the gang, who all pled guilty. Miller received a ten-year sentence, Evans two years, and Williams one year.[16]

Fountain did not stop there. One source claims that before the year was out he had sent twenty rustlers to the penitentiary.[17] The *Rio Grande Republican* reported that Fountain "sent no less than fifteen cattle thieves to the penitentiary for terms of up to ten years."[18] During this time, Fountain remained active in the Republican Party. The 1894 elections brought more trouble and added to the Fountain-Fall feud. Both sides had watched the polls closely that election. Still, allegations from both parties of stolen ballot boxes, discarded and duplicated ballots, and voter registration fraud followed. Recounts were presided over by none other than District Judge Albert B. Fall. Two key seats were contested. One was for a seat on the state legislature. Republican nominee Albert Fountain (Albert J. Fountain's son) was originally declared the winner by over two hundred votes, but Democrat Pinito Piño was declared the winner after the final tally. The other seat in question, which would have a significant impact on future events, was for the office of sheriff.

One incident of alleged fraud involved a box of eighty-eight ballots that disappeared during lunch and later turned up in the post office, all marked Democrat. Without these votes, the winner for sheriff would have been Republican Numa Reymond. The votes were allowed and Democrat Guadalupe Ascarate was declared the winner. Fountain and the Republicans appealed. It was still in the courts when Fountain disappeared.[19]

In February 1895, in the wake of seemingly partisan actions as a judge during the 1894 elections, Albert Fall was asked for and submitted his resignation as judge of the Third Judicial District Court. Fall returned to his law practice and mining. With Judge Fall's resignation, Lee, Gililland, and McNew lost their commission as U. S. Deputy marshals. No matter, since new sheriff Ascarate appointed them deputies.[20]

Oliver Milton Lee was born in Burnet County, Texas, on October 31, 1865. Growing up on a ranch, he was a natural with horses. He was described as good looking and charming. He did not smoke or drink. Lee came to New Mexico with a herd of horses and went into ranching. Albert Fall took an instant liking to this young man and a close friendship grew.[21] Historian C. L. Sonnichsen described Lee like this: "He had one great urge—he wanted to get ahead. He had one great talent—he was a natural shot."[22]

James Robert Gililland was born in Brown, Texas, on July 26, 1872. The family moved to New Mexico when Jim was thirteen. He worked on various ranches, including the Oliver Lee ranch. Gililland was tall, lanky, and good-looking. He was also known to drink.[23]

William McNew was born in Texas on May 8, 1864. He married Nettie Fry on June 17, 1889, in Hillsboro, New Mexico.[24] Sonnichsen described McNew as "a tough Texan with ice-blue eyes"[25] and Historian Katie Stoes said he was "considered an all-round bad man."[26]

Fountain, meanwhile, was moving in on a gang said to be headed by Oliver Lee, and included fellow deputies James Gililland and William McNew. They were suspected of stealing cattle and altering brands.[27] On October 3, 1895, Fountain wrote to James Cree. The letter told of some of Fountain's plans and what they were up against. It began, "I have to communicate to you matters of the most grave importance, seriously affecting the interest of all honest stock growers in this country, and especially in the vicinity of Tularosa. I had perhaps better begin at the beginning, and state the facts in detail chronologically."

Fountain wrote that he "had Williams, Cormack and others at work in the vicinity of Tularosa and La Luz and soon obtained positive evidence that a man named Dodd was running a butcher shop at Tularosa, and was killing all the cattle that came in his way . . . ." He said that one of the gang, a man named Williams, "was induced to peach, and through him" they "learned that Oliver Lee and others of the Fall party were connected with the thieves and this will account for what subsequently occurred." Fountain was confidant that they had obtained "sufficient evidence" to secure the indictments "of all the parties by any unprejudiced grand jury, especially in one case of the killing of a V pitchfork V animal by Dodd, the eye witnesses being at hand to testify as to the stealing and killing." They were also able to prove "that in a small valley over one hundred animals had been killed by these parties." Fountain continued, "It being impossible to prevent these facts from obtaining publicity, the gang of criminals soon became acquainted with our intentions and became desperate, threats were made against Williams, myself and all others connected with the proposed prosecutions; this culminated in the shooting of Williams by Fall and Morgan in the streets of Las Cruces."[28]

The shooting of Deputy Ben Williams happened when, for reasons not clear, Fall, Joe Morgan, and a third man opened fire on Williams. Williams returned fire, hitting Morgan in the arm. A shot from Fall passed through Williams' hat, and another shot from Morgan hit Williams in the left elbow and exited his shoulder.[29] Fountain wrote:

> I was anonymously notified, that if I attempted to prosecute these parties I would be killed. Of course I paid no attention to these threats. When the grand jury convened we found that a large majority were tools of Fall; the Hon. George W. Miles, being the foreman, we had when the Grand Jury met nine men in jail charged with cattle stealing. Dodd was under arrest awaiting the action of the jury; the witnesses against him were present; instead of investigating these cases, the Grand Jury proceeded to investigate Williams and myself, Fall went before the Grand Jury and swore that the stock association had paid men to assassinate him, and sixteen of his satellites

on the grand jury did as he wished; there was no investigation of any of the jail cases. Williams was indicted for murder (killing a criminal he was attempting to arrest about a year ago) and some other indictments were found against him in connection with his arrest of Dick Wilson at Clayton (charged by J. H. Riley with horse stealing). I was honored by an indictment charging me with forging a private telegram to myself from Major Tell of El Paso some years ago, saying, "I will send you papers first mail." The message from Tell to me of course was genuine; was our private business, and concerned nobody but ourselves; nevertheless, this ridiculous charge was made by the Grand Jury; the indictment was immediately dismissed by Judge Bantz when it came into court, and he read Mr. Miles a lecture on the subject . . . . Williams is still in bed seriously wounded. Fall admits he shot him; the grand jury reported they could not find time to investigate this shooting. I learn from the inside that the gang we are after are making threats against many of the association members, and especially against yourself.

I shall now begin to fight this gang in earnest. I require funds and immediately upon receipt of your check for the quarter beginning September 1st I shall start in person for Tularosa, and begin the work of corraling [*sic*] this entire gang. I find that they have no public sentiment to sustain them there or at La Luz. While I entertain no serious apprehension of any attempt on the part of the Tularosa gang to execute their threats against yourself, yet I advise prudence on your part should you be compelled to visit any place where there may be danger of encountering them, and it would be advisable to always travel in company with some person on whom you can rely in an emergency.

It was unfortunate that Fountain did not heed his own advice and always travel in the company of someone he could rely on. He closed the letter:

> My family affairs have occasioned me very great anxiety and trouble; the shock of her mother's death had greatly affected Mrs. Fountain, and her illness is aggravated by mental trouble arising from her apprehension that my life is in danger. I entertain no such apprehension, yet were I to so believe, I should not be deterred thereby from performing my whole duty. Public opinion here is with us, and the present condition of affairs cannot long exist, nevertheless, I anticipate a hard contest, one perhaps to the death.[30]

Did Fountain correctly anticipate that this would be the death of him? This letter would later be used to implicate suspects and show motive for his murder. Just as he did other times in his life, this brave man would not let fear deter him from what he felt needed to be done.

Les Dow obtained the evidence he needed against Lee when he investigated Lee's herd. Dow had two cowboys, George Bunting and Lee Green, butcher a steer from the herd. When the carcass was examined from the inside, it showed that the original brand had been altered and changed to Lee's brand. Lee was not present at the time but Dow was able to arrest Lee's cowhand William McNew. After making bond, McNew went with a posse including deputies Lee and Gililland and arrested Bunting and Green. Bunting and

Green, who were only acting on Dow's orders, were nonetheless charged with unlawfully killing and skinning a steer belonging to Lee and McNew. They were each released on $1,000 bond.[31]

William H. H. Llewellyn
(Date and photographer unknown.
Courtesy Palace of the Governors
[MNM/DCA], Negative No. 7607)

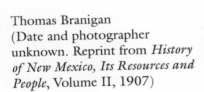

Thomas Branigan
(Date and photographer
unknown. Reprint from *History
of New Mexico, Its Resources and
People*, Volume II, 1907)

three

The Disappearance

On January 12, 1896, Albert J. Fountain left for Lincoln, but he did not leave alone. The rumors of an attempt on his life worried his family. Family members, especially Fountain's easily alarmed wife Mariana, attempted to persuade him to cancel the trip, or at least not go alone. Family recollections disagree on whether it was Fountain's wife Mariana or daughter Maggie who had the idea that he take his youngest son Henry. Mariana certainly pushed the idea, thinking that no attempt would be made on her husband's life when a child was with him. She finally won out and Fountain agreed that if Henry was home from school when he left, he would take him. Henry returned home in time and went on what must have been an exciting trip for a young boy to take with his father.[1]

The Fountain family received a scare the first night when Fountain's horses arrived back home. Later, a miner who came to town delivered a note from Colonel Fountain saying that the horses had run away. Fountain's son Albert, along with his father-in-law Antonio Garcia, brought the horses back to the colonel and he and Henry were able to continue.[2]

The father and son travelled 150 miles, through the desert, past the White Sands, and to the town of Lincoln, located high in the Capitan Mountains, where the ground was likely covered in snow. The courthouse in Lincoln was the same building from which Billy the Kid had made his famous escape fifteen years earlier.

In court, with the assistance of Fountain, the prosecution presented evidence such as brand registration documents, letters, affidavits, depositions, and the altered cowhide. The jury came back with thirty-two indictments against twenty-three men. Included were case No. 1489-Territory of New Mexico vs. William "McNue" (McNew) and Oliver Lee; Charge-Larceny of cattle and case No. 1890-Territory of New Mexico vs. William McNue and Oliver Lee; Charge-Defacing brands.[3]

On January 30, as Fountain stepped out of the courthouse, he was anonymously given a note. It simply said: "If you drop this we will be your friends. If you go on with it you will never reach home alive."[4]

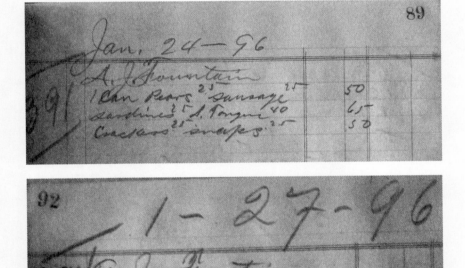

Colonel Fountain's entry and pencil signatures in ledger books of store in Lincoln, January 24, 1896 and January 27, 1896 (possibly his last signature before his death).
(Photograph by author, 2004. Books in possession of and permission to photograph and publish given by Lincoln State Monument.)

Lincoln County Courthouse, circa 1930. (Author's collection)

Probably the last man to speak to Fountain in Lincoln was attorney George Pritchard, who urged him to wait until the mail carrier made the trip from Lincoln the next day and to go with him. Fountain, not following his own advice to James Cree, declined. He and Henry left Lincoln and headed west. It was the dead of winter and would take three days to reach home.[5]

They spent the first night at the home of Joseph Blazer at Blazer's Mill. Blazer's Mill was a sawmill located on but not a part of the Mescalero Apache Reservation. In addition to the lumber the mill produced, Blazer was also a licensed trader on the Mescalero reservation.[6] That night as they talked, Fountain told Joseph Blazer that they had enough evidence to convict, provided the gang didn't make away with Fountain or the witnesses.[7]

The next morning, an Apache friend gave Fountain a pony as part of a debt he owed him. Fountain accepted the pony for his children, tied it to the back of the buckboard, and continued.[8] During the day, Fountain noticed two men on horseback who seemed to be trailing him. Sometimes they were in front of him and sometimes behind him. They were always off the road and never close enough to identify.

Albert and Henry spent that night at the home of David Sutherland in La Luz. While there, Fountain gave his son a quarter to go spend at Myer's store. Henry bought ten cents' worth of candy and tied the dime and nickel of change in the corner of his handkerchief.

The pair left early on a windy and cold Saturday morning. Fountain now saw three horsemen following and watching them. Again, sometimes the horsemen were ahead, sometimes behind. One of the men was on a white horse and the other two on darker horses. One wore a black hat and the others light ones. They were never close enough to identify. Fountain spoke briefly with mail carrier Santos Alvarado in the morning hours. Albert and Henry ate lunch at Pellman's Well then continued west past the White Sands. A few hours after lunch they met five riders on the road. One of them was Saturnino Barela, a mail carrier whom Fountain knew. They exchanged a few pleasantries, then the conversation turned to the three horsemen. Barela asked Fountain to go with him and spend the night at Luna's Well. Fountain's actions showed that he was more concerned with not worrying Mariana by keeping her waiting than he was with the unidentified horsemen. He thanked Barela but declined the invitation, saying his wife was expecting the pair for dinner. Also, Henry was coming down with a cold and needed his mother's care. Barela watched the two ride off.[9]

Albert and Henry probably sat close, with Henry covered in his Indian blanket, to keep warm from the frigid wind. Father and son rode towards the warm home that was waiting for them in Mesilla, a home they would never see again.

Saturnino Barela returned down the same road the next morning, this time heading towards Las Cruces. Barela was about five miles past the spot where he had met Fountain the previous day when he noticed that the tracks of the colonel's buckboard turned off the road just past Chalk Hill, which the road cut through. Barela, remembering their conversation and the horsemen from the

White Sands, dusk.
(Author's photograph, 2002)

Henry Fountain (left) with his grandmother, Maria de Jesus Perez, and cousin, Tomas Perez. Circa 1893
(Date and photographer unknown. Courtesy New Mexico State University Library, Archives and Special Collections, Mary Alexander papers, RG88-056.)

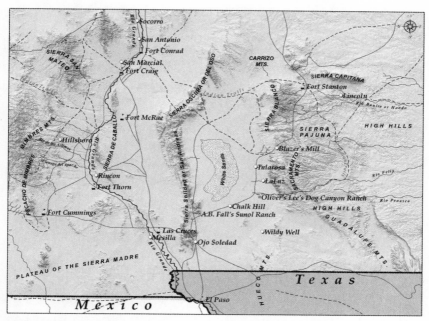

Key Sites
(Map by Linda Wimberly)

previous day, suspected that something was wrong. He followed the tracks thirty to forty yards. Upon examining them, he found the tracks of the colonel's buggy and horses plus the tracks of three other horses. The concerned friend hurried to Las Cruces.[10]

The Fountain family was expecting the pair home early Sunday. The tension in the household grew with each passing hour. That evening, as Mariana, with most of the family at the house, waited for her husband and son, Barela knocked at the door. The colonel's eldest son Albert answered. Barela asked for Colonel Fountain and upon being told that he had not arrived home, Barela related the story of seeing him and Henry the day before, and told of the tracks he had seen that morning. There can be no doubt of how the family must have felt.

At once Albert, with his brother Jack and father-in-law Antonio Garcia, formed a posse of townsmen and raced off into the cold and windy night for Chalk Hill. Later that night another, better organized, posse left town to join in the search. This posse, led by Major William Llewellyn, consisted of about twenty-five persons and included former Doña Ana County sheriff Captain Eugene Van Patten and Captain Thomas Branigan. Both posses joined forces the next morning.[11]

Once at Chalk Hill they made discoveries. Imprints of a man kneeling behind a bush were found. Two empty cartridges were nearby. The posse believed that the man behind the bush had held up Fountain while two other horsemen charged out. The buckboard swerved off road and the horsemen followed it, racing a hundred yards or so before they stopped. The evidence, such as hoof prints, footprints, and cigarette papers, suggested they stopped for some time. Back by the roadside a pool of blood would later be found, not by this search group because sleet covered the ground, but from the next party to come through a week to ten days later. The blood was splattered over an area six feet across. It appeared that a blanket was laid beside the stain and a heavy object placed upon it. Bits of wool were in the sand as was the mark of the weave of a blanket. The posse deduced that Fountain was shot where the buckboard had first left the road. Blood had built up in his overcoat and when the buckboard veered, Fountain fell off to the right and the blood splattered as he hit the ground. Nearby a blood-soaked handkerchief and two powder-burned coins, a nickel and a dime, were found.[12]

That afternoon the posse came across the abandoned buck-board at the red sand dunes, twelve miles from Chalk Hill. Again, there appeared to be the tracks of three distinct horses and three distinct sets of boots. Branigan measured the tracks, breaking sticks to measure the length and depth of the tracks. Llewellyn measured them with a pocket ruler. Again, they found the imprint of a blanket that appeared to have a heavy object resting on it. The buckboard was plundered of most of Fountain's possessions. A valise and boxes had been opened and their contents were either missing or scattered around. Missing were all of the papers regarding the indictments Fountain had secured in Lincoln.[13] Other missing items included Fountain's Winchester rifle, a dagger, a canteen, a lap robe, an Indian blanket, and a quilt.[14] Two straps from the harnesses of Fountain's horses were missing. Posse members speculated that the straps could have been used to tie the bodies on the horses.[15] The warning note Fountain received in Lincoln was left in the buckboard. Fountain's tie was hanging on a wheel spoke. Under the seat, neatly folded, was a *rebozo* (scarf). Henry's little hat was still in the valise.[16]

From there, the posse followed the trail about another five miles, to an apparent campsite, where they found the remains of a campfire. Signs showed that horses were fed oats and that a meal of bacon and coffee had been cooked. There was also a broken whisky bottle. Branigan, an expert tracker, identified the tracks as the same ones found at the last site. One clue was a boot track with a run-over heel. They again carefully measured the tracks. There was also the blanket imprint, again with the signs of a heavy weight being placed upon it. Then they found footprints of a child's shoe. Four tracks led about six feet from the campfire. Albert identified them as Henry's. Unfortunately, it was the right shoe only. It was speculated that the shoe had either been attached to a stick or by hand pressed into the sand, possibly to confuse or toy with anyone who followed.[17] A son and brother brought false hope from this finding, as Jack Fountain told the *El Paso Times*, "I think that owing to the presence of my little brother, father must have surrendered rather than have the little boy hurt."[18] Jack would tell the *Santa Fe New Mexican* two weeks later that he believed his father and brother were dead.[19]

The posse followed the trail east and came to a point where it branched off in three directions. Carl Clausen and Luis Herrera took the trail that went southeast into the Jarilla Mountains. Van

Patten took a group of men west. Llewellyn led the main party northeast towards the Sacramento Mountains. That night a fresh snow fell on the men. At dawn, Llewellyn moved on with Lew Gans, John Casey, Thomas Branigan, and Henry Stoes, and sent the rest of his group back to Las Cruces with the buckboard.[20]

Van Patten's posse found a horse that had been one of Fountain's buckboard team. The horse had dried blood matted on its left side, and its back was sore, apparently from carrying a heavy load.[21]

Llewellyn's posse followed a trail that to Llewellyn, and most others of the posse, seemed to lead towards Oliver Lee's Dog Canyon ranch. They would never know for certain because as they neared the ranch, being only a few miles away, a herd of cattle driven by two of Lee's cowboys passed in front of them and destroyed the trail. The men said they were taking the cattle to Lee's Wildy Well ranch. The posse in turn headed towards Wildy Well to water their horses. The name Wildy came from the well's previous owner. Meanwhile, the set of tracks Clausen and Herrera were following led them directly to Wildy Well.[22]

The tracks they were following appeared to have been made at night, as the horse that made the tracks had run straight into mesquite bushes more then once. When Lee's hands saw the riders approach the ranch, they scattered so that when Clausen and Herrera reached the house no one was in site.

The first man to come out of the house was Ed, a black ranch hand who, according to Clausen, was "stepping sideways, in his hand a six-shooter." He stepped slowly until he was past Clausen and then made a dash behind the water tank. The next man came out. Clausen spoke to him, but received no answer. Oliver Lee came out next. Clausen asked him if he and Herrera could fill their water kegs. Lee said they could and told them to get the water. Lee asked Clausen what they were doing and Clausen told him they were searching for the Fountains. Clausen then asked if Lee and his men could go out and assist them. Lee responded that he hadn't time and "what the hell are those sons of bitches to us?" With that, Lee mounted his horse and left, heading towards the Jarilla Mountains.

When Lee fell out of sight, Clausen examined the tracks of his horse and found them to be the same that he had followed. Moments later, when paying for the water, Clausen would see McNew in the ranch house.[23]

Oliver M. Lee (Date and photographer unknown. Courtesy of University of Texas at El Paso Library, Special Collections Department, C. L. Sonnichsen papers, No. 141-62-73-541.)

four

Pat Garrett Summoned

As the search parties returned, the newspapers ran with the story. Under the headline "Were They Murdered?" the February 4 edition of the *El Paso Times* reported, "Yesterday El Paso's pleasant little neighbor, Las Cruces, was in a tempest of excitement over a report to the effect that Col. A. J. Fountain, of that town, and his little eight-year-old son had been murdered by unknown parties . . . ." The article went on to quote Ben Williams, who told the paper, "That's what a man gets for prosecuting cattle thieves in New Mexico."[1]

The next day, the *Santa Fe New Mexican* ran the headline "No Trace Of Col. Fountain," and, under the heading "Parental Solicitude," editorialized:

> no doubt is entertained that the lips of Col. Fountain and his son have since been stilled forever by their cruel and vengeful captors on the theory that "dead men tell no tales." Of course there could be no motive for murdering the child except to put a dangerous witness out of the way . . . . God grant that the dark mystery that shrouds this awful, this hideous, this unspeakably cowardly crime may be lifted, and that at least the fiends incarnate who perpetrated it may be discovered and punished in accordance with the enormity of their offense.[2]

The *Socorro Chieftain* said,

> The murder of Col. Fountain and his little son is the work of fiends and they should be exterminated just the same as you would go after a band of wolves, once their identity is established. We do not want anyone to understand that we are in favor of lynch law. Not by any means, but we believe that these murderers should be hunted down, their identity established, and the shortest road to the gallows should be taken.[3]

New Mexico citizens were outraged. This was just another example of the lawlessness that ran rampant throughout the territory, a primary reason why statehood was continually delayed.

To further complicate matters was the impression that the sheriff's office of Las Cruces would be utterly useless, as the seat was still contested and the acting sheriff, Guadalupe Ascarate, was said to be a puppet of Albert B. Fall. Furthermore, Ascarate's deputies Oliver Lee, Jim Gililland, William McNew, Joe Morgan, and Jack Tucker, were all becoming suspects in the Fountain disappearance.[4]

Fall's *Independent Democrat* speculated that Fountain might still be alive, that he had just left New Mexico for a new life. It published reports that Fountain had been seen in St. Louis, San Francisco, Chicago, New York, and Denver. Rumors circulated and articles hinted that Fountain had taken his favorite son and run off with a younger woman.[5] Fall told the *El Paso Herald*, "it remained to be found out whether there had been any murder as claimed."[6]

Upon hearing he was suspected in the Fountain murder, Oliver Lee came up to Las Cruces but was told there was no evidence against him. While in town, Lee told a *Rio Grande Republican* reporter that he did not believe Colonel Fountain was dead.[7]

As the bad press mounted, there was pressure on the governor to have the case settled and to bring in someone who would actually go after the murderers. Governor Thornton took quick action. Thornton, as well as many private citizens and groups including the Masonic lodges, the county of Doña Ana, and Roswell citizens offered rewards.[8] Then came the question of who would go after the killers. An outsider was needed who would not get caught up in the politics that weakened the incumbent office. Governor Thornton called on Pat Garrett.

Patrick Floyd Garrett was born on June 5, 1850, in Chambers, Alabama, but spent most of his youth in Louisiana. Moving west, Garrett worked variously as a ranch hand and a buffalo hunter, spending much of the time in Texas and then in New Mexico. On the heels of the Lincoln County War, with New Mexico in anarchy, prominent New Mexico citizens including John Chisum asked Garrett to move from Fort Sumner to Roswell in time to run in the November 1880 election for sheriff of Lincoln County. Garrett, a Democrat, won his party's nomination and then the election. As the sheriff of Lincoln County, Garrett gained his place in history as the man who killed Billy the Kid on July 14, 1881. He served only one term in office, not being re-elected after the violence in Lincoln Country subsided. Garrett turned to ranching. Struggling financially, and with his fifth child on the way, he jumped at the opportunity offered by Governor Thornton in 1896.[9]

Garrett, who was living in Uvalde, Texas, met with Governor Thornton in El Paso. The bipartisan meeting in Thornton's hotel room included Fall, Llewellyn, George Curry, Reymond, and Ascarate. The purpose of the meeting was to settle the ongoing dispute over the sheriff's office. Reymond offered to drop the lawsuit if Ascarate would resign as sheriff, which would clear the way for Thornton to appoint Garrett to the post. Fall, on behalf of Ascarate, flatly refused, claiming that this was all politics. Thornton then asked Ascarate to hire Garrett as his chief deputy and allow him to work on the Fountain case, but Ascarate refused, saying "that he was able to take care of the sheriff's office and would not let anybody dictate who his deputies should be." [10] The meeting ended without accomplishment. An editorial in the *Roswell Record* said of Fall's actions in the meeting: "Fall objected on the grounds that Garrett's appointment would be an admission that the sheriff was unable to cope with the lawlessness now rampant in that country. There was another objection which did not come to the surface, but which can be seen, and that is, Garrett would probably unearth the murderers of Colonel Fountain and his little son."[11]

Two days after the meeting in El Paso, Thornton offered to hire Garrett as a private detective until the sheriff's contest was settled. Garrett took the job in hopes that he would eventually become sheriff.[12] In a letter to his wife, his motives for taking the job were clear. He told her that the sheriff's office would be worth $6,000 a year and he would receive an additional $8,000 with the arrest and conviction of the Fountain murderers. He wrote the wife he dearly missed, "You know, if it were not that we are so poor, I would not be away from you a minute, so, if I am successful we will get located in this country, and I will never be away from you and the children again."[13] Garrett did eventually move his family to Las Cruces.

In the meantime, he began speaking to people familiar with the case, talking to those who had, or thought they had, relevant information, interviewing witnesses, visiting the sites, and searching for the bodies, often with Sheriff Charles C. Perry of Roswell.[14] A hot-tempered forty-one or forty-two-year-old former Texan, Perry would spend much time assisting Garrett in the first months of the Fountain case.[15] Garrett met with the Fountain family. Garrett wrote that he had never seen such a distressed family. "People think Mrs. Fountain and one of his daughters will go crazy."[16]

One piece of evidence Garrett received around this time was the testimony of Eva Taylor. It is unknown if this undated statement which appears to be in Ben Williams's handwriting was the particular statement Garrett received. Nevertheless, it contained the same general information, according to another report by a Pinkerton operative.[17]

Eva Taylor stated that on the night of February 1, 1896, she took the stage from a ranch near the White Sands and headed east. At about 2 a.m., when they were about twenty miles from La Luz, she saw a large fire near La Luz that appeared to be about ten miles from the road. Taylor switched to another stage and proceeded with the stage driven by Alvino Guerra. They passed through La Luz at daylight and a few miles past, while heading towards Tularosa, they saw three horsemen coming from the direction of where the fire had earlier been seen. According to Taylor, the horsemen did not ride directly toward the stage and they appeared not to want to be seen. Taylor told Williams, "I recognized two of the men as being Oliver Lee and Billy McNew. The third man I think was Frank Chatfield but am not certain. I am well acquainted with Lee and McNew . . . ."[18] Garrett did not believe her.[19]

There is more testimony Williams's hand, unfortunately undated, in which witnesses were able to identify suspects. The following statements could have been made between the years 1896 and 1900, but were most likely made early in the investigation to either Pat Garrett or Ben Williams. A statement in Williams's handwriting reported that José Hermosillo and Antonio (last name illegible) had seen Colonel Fountain at Cherokee Bill Spring. The pair also saw Jack Tucker and William Carr on the road near Dog Canyon. They said that Tucker and Carr appeared to be on the lookout and rode off when Fountain came in sight.[20] Luis Garcia, a stage driver, repeated this.[21]

There was more information on Tucker and Carr. On Friday, Adam Dieter and others had seen them in Tularosa. They were said to have watched Colonel Fountain. Jack Tucker was seen on the road by William Bailey and a Mrs. McDonald, both of whom stated that Tucker turned his head to avoid being recognized and that he was riding at full speed. Tucker and Carr were seen by others watching Fountain that day at La Luz.[22] It was said that after the murder, Carr "told at Tularosa that Fountain would never again prosecute small cattle men."

A man named Paul James and his wife stated that "Lee and McNew said they would kill any man who would attempt to prosecute them."[23]

An important statement came from Jack Maxwell, who would have trouble remembering it all later on. Maxwell, who was at the time working for James Cree, went to Dog Canyon on the day of the disappearance. Oliver Lee was not there, but Lee's mother told Maxwell "the boys were out hunting stock and would return that night . . . ." Maxwell said "they did not return until Sunday when they rode up to the house on fresh looking horses . . . ." They acted suspicious of Maxwell. Shortly after they arrived, Maxwell went out a short distance from the house and found where "they had changed horses and the horses they had brought in were ridden down and looked as if they had been ridden all night . . ." Oliver Lee's mother, however, "told Mrs. McDonald that Oliver could not have had any hand in the killing of Fountain that he and the boys were at Dog Cañon [Canyon]."[24]

On March 1, Garrett visited the murder site.[25] As he and Perry searched for the Fountain bodies and sought information, Governor Thornton brought in further help.

Pat Garrett, 1898.
(Photographer unknown. Courtesy University of Texas at El Paso Library, Special Collections Department, Doña Ana County Sheriffs photograph collection, PH005-1-10 DUP.)

five

Bring in the Pinkertons

Shortly after Pat Garrett began his work on the case, Governor Thornton brought in additional help. Garrett was a man of action, a man who could round up the suspected parties. What Thornton sought next was a professional investigator. He called in the Pinkertons.

The Pinkerton National Detective Agency had been founded in 1850 by Scottish immigrant Allan Pinkerton. For years, Pinkerton men served as ruthless strikebreakers and bodyguards, most notably for President Lincoln. Pinkerton private detectives also pursued some of the most wanted men in the West, among them the James and Younger gangs, the Hole-in-the-Wall gang, Butch Cassidy and the Sundance Kid, and the Wild Bunch.[1]

Thornton contacted the Pinkertons towards the end of February. It had been worked out ahead of time with James Cree that their investigation would be paid for by the Southeastern New Mexico Stock Growers' Association. Cree also sent Thornton the letter he received from Colonel Fountain, dated October 3, 1895, showing Fountain was aware of threats against his life.[2]

On February 28 James McParland, head of the Denver office of the Pinkertons, wrote Governor Thornton that he would send out two men: one at that time, who would make an open investigation, and after him, another man known only to Thornton.[3] The first man McParland sent was his assistant, John C. Fraser. Fraser was born to Scottish parents in Chicago, Illinois, on March 31, 1860. After working variously as a clerk, a plumber, and a printer, Fraser was hired by the Pinkerton National Detective Agency on June 28, 1880. He began working from the Chicago office, but eventually moved west to the Denver office. The married detective's employment records describe his physical appearance as five-foot nine inches tall, with a slight build and dark complexion.

Fraser left Denver for Santa Fe on March 2 and arrived at 1:10 a.m. the morning of the fourth.[4] He went to the governor's office early that morning. Thornton was not feeling well so he did not arrive when expected, but when he did arrive, he and Fraser discussed the Fountain case.

Fraser learned from Governor Thornton that Colonel Fountain was last seen by the mail driver Saturnino Barela on February 1, 1896, between 3:00 and 4:00 p.m. about forty miles north of Las Cruces. Thornton told Fraser that Barela saw three mounted men too far from the road to recognize. Thornton drew a map of the area where Fountain's buckboard left the road. Fraser wrote in his report:

> I was also informed that Col. Fountain had disappeared once before in very mysterious manner for fifteen days and then showed up again. He is said to be of sensational disposition but in this case there was every reason to believe that he and son, seven or eight years of age, were both dead. He had many enemies, owing to his position as attorney for [the] stock growers association, he had always been a bitter prosecutor of cattle thieves and was a fearless man . . . The parties who are suspected of this crime are, Oliver Lee, William McNew, James Gilliland [Gililland], or Jack Tucker, all cattlemen. The men for me to meet at Las Cruces who are interested in

this case are Major W. H. H. Lewellyn [Llewellyn], S. B. Newcomb, and A. L. Christie [Christy]; all these men are Masons and are interested in running this matter down.

After lunch, Thornton and Fraser met again and Fraser was given letters of introduction to Llewellyn, Christy, and District Attorney Young. Fraser wrote of Young: "The latter is not to be trusted but I will call on him and learn what I can."[5]

John Fraser arrived in Las Cruces the morning of Thursday, March 5, 1896. He went directly to the Rio Grande Hotel, which he noted was the only one in town. Fraser first sought out Major Llewellyn, but learned that he was not in town. Fraser's next stop was the law office of Albert L. Christy, where he spoke to Christy and a man named Curran.

After discussing Fountain's trip from Lincoln until his disappearance, Fraser was told of Joe Morgan, a deputy U. S. marshal, "who is said to be closely connected with Ex-Judge A. B. Fell [Fall], Oliver Lee, McNew and other cattle thieves." Fraser was told that Morgan was said to have gone to Tularosa to make an arrest at about the time that court opened at Lincoln. Morgan did arrest a woman at Tularosa, but sent another man to bring her in while he remained at Tularosa. As soon as Fountain arrived, Morgan left and went east towards Lincoln, "but he must have circled around for he arrived in Las Cruces on Saturday, February 1st, about 4 p. m." which, as Fraser noted, was about the time Barela met Fountain on the road. Fraser wrote:

> this of course would let Morgan out as one of the actual parties to the murder, but would not prevent him from notifying others of the arrival of the Col. Morgan is considered a very bad man and goes armed to the teeth, as do several others of the same gang,

all of whom are said to be controlled by Ex-Judge A. B. Fell. This man Fell has always been the attorney for these cattle thieves and is said to be tied up with them now. He disliked Col. Fountain very much and seemed to consider him his arch enemy . . . .

Christy told Fraser "Colonel Fountain had some 22 indictments against the suspected parties at the time of his disappearance . . . ."

They then discussed the Fountain family. Fraser was told that the Fountains were "considered very nice people." Mrs. Fountain was said to be somewhat jealous of her husband, "but as near as Mr. Christie or Mr. Curran know there was no trouble between them at the time he went away . . . ."

Shortly after 6:00, Fraser returned to the hotel and had supper. Afterwards Fraser, undercover, sat in the hotel lobby to listen and see what he might learn.[6] He would do this in the lobby, in saloons, and at shops through out his investigation to see what information he could pick up.[7]

The next day Fraser met several men he considered key to the investigation. His notes read:

> Today in Las Cruces,—
>
> After breakfast I wrote up my reports and then called upon Mr. A. L. Christy (not Christie) at his office. I wanted to get several names and locations mentioned by him correct. I learned that Dist. Atty. Young was at El Paso as was also Ex-Judge A. B. Fall (not Fell. [sic] Major Lewellyn was expected up from El Paso today at noon and Mr. Christy was going to the depot to meet him . . . .

Fraser went with Christy to meet Llewellyn. From there, he went with Llewellyn to his house. Fraser noted, "As Major Lewellyn has been over the ground he will be able to give me a good drawing of the road, etc." Fraser left for lunch then returned.

Fraser reported, "I was informed that the sheriff and deputies all went armed to the teeth and were all under the orders of A. B. Fall and that every move made by the men interested in running down this matter was closely watched and that Joe Morgan, the ex-deputy marshal mentioned in my report of yesterday and who is now a deputy sheriff, his commission as U. S. deputy marshal having been taken away, has openly threatened some of the best men in town, claiming that they have been talking too much about this Fountain case."[8]

Major Llewellyn, who was already obviously convinced Fall and "the gang" were responsible for Fountain's murder, continued to discuss how these deputies had harassed, threatened, and even planned to kill Llewellyn and some of the others interested in the case. Llewellyn gave a number of examples and gave "the name of a negro barber named [Albert] Ellis" that Llewellyn said was "the right hand man" of Fall. According to Llewellyn, Ellis was "said to have been a hard character back in Texas where he had committed more than one crime." Llewellyn said Ellis was "very prominent in dogging the movements" of himself and others.

While they discussed the case, Judge McFie came to see Llewellyn. Fraser, who could see that McFie wanted to speak to Llewellyn alone, excused himself. When he had left the building, Llewellyn also came out and told him that McFie had received a letter in the mail warning him that he was to be killed. The letter was not signed, but the writer said that the judge had done him a favor while on the bench and he wanted to warn him. Fraser then left. When he returned, Llewellyn told Fraser that owing to the language in the letter and the remark about McFie having done the writer a favor, McFie thought the man who wrote the letter was the barber Albert Ellis, for McFie had loaned him sixty dollars at one time.

Llewellyn then picked up where he had left off before the interruption. He stated "that these men, towit:—Fall, McNew, Lee, Ellis, Morgan, Tucker and many others are banded into an oath bond organized body . . . ." Llewellyn told Fraser that a short time ago Fall, who was then a judge, had sent for him through Tom Baird. When they arrived, Fall had told Llewellyn and Baird that the Democratic Party wanted the two with them. At this time, Llewellyn "had sort of broken away from the party as certain things had happened which he did not like." Fall told Llewellyn and Baird "that the Democratic party must carry this territory." Llewellyn said "this was impossible, but Fall said it was not as they were banded together like brothers and if any of them got in trouble they could furnish any kind of evidence to clear them." When they left, Llewellyn asked Baird "what he thought of it," to which Baird responded, "If that is Democratic politics I don't want any of it." It was never brought up again.

Llewellyn next described the Ben Williams shooting:

> Only a short time ago Fall tried to kill a man named [Ben] Williams on the street in this town, shot him twice. We have had eleven murders here and no convictions. Oliver Lee, McNew, Tucker, and the balance of the gang are all deputies under the present sheriff and several cold blooded murders are credited up to Oliver Lee and his friends McNew, Tucker and others. All of these killings they claim was done in self defense, but in each case Oliver Lee jumped the ranch of the man he killed.

Fraser noted, "I find everybody very timid about here and for this reason my work is going to be very slow. No one wishes to be connected with me or the case openly, so you can see from this how the feeling stands."[9]

It was an ugly state of affairs that Fraser described. Case in point was Fraser's meeting that night with the mail driver Barela. To protect Barela, the meeting took place in the back of a general store, with Llewellyn, his son Morgan, and Thomas Branigan acting as lookouts.

Barela, with the storeowner Freudenthal acting as translator, repeated what he had already told others. He was riding along with a group of four others who joined him a few miles behind. Barela stated that when he met Colonel Fountain and Henry they were around two and a half miles east of Chalk Hill traveling towards Las Cruces. Barela saw the three horsemen about a half-mile ahead of Colonel Fountain. He said of the horsemen, "they were not nearer to us than a quarter of a mile at any time for they turned from the road when they saw us. We could not identify any of them from that distance, but one rode a white horse and the others dark horses and one wore a black hat and the others light . . . ."

Barela and Fountain had some small talk, which quickly turned to the three men. Fountain asked Barela if he knew who they were. Barela said, "I could see that the Colonel was uneasy, and I told him he could turn back to the station and stop over night and then come through with me on the next day." Fountain thought it over a while and then said, "No I guess I will push along." He then left at a "brisk rate."

Barela stated that on his way back over the road the following day he watched the colonel's tracks from the point where they had talked. Past Chalk Hill, Barela saw where Fountain's tracks left the road. He exited his buckboard and followed the tracks about thirty or forty yards. Barela said that at that point, "I saw the tracks of other horses and then I feared the worst." Upon his arrival in town, Barela informed others of what he had seen.

Barela said that the man who took the mail from him at Luna's Well, one Santos Alvarado, had since seen two or three men riding along the road, evidently watching it. "It is his opinion that these men are watching to see if the bodies are found and he thinks they are buried close by where the Colonel's buggy was found. (This of course is only his opinion)."[10]

The next day Fraser spoke further with William Llewellyn and received from him information about Fall's actions the days leading up to and on the day of Fountain's murder. According to Llewellyn, Fall left Las Cruces on the day before the murder for his Sunol property, where he had a mine. On the afternoon of the murder, Fall left Sunol for Las Cruces. "Now Fall claims that he got here [Las Cruces] about 6 p.m. or a little after dark, but this is not so, as he was met by a Mr. Cox on the road from Sunol after half past eight driving like the old Harry . . . . Now the distance from Las Cruces to Sunol is about 25 miles and from Chalk Creek [Hill] to Sunol is about 14 to 16 miles straight across and I am told that you can see the clothes on the line in Cowan's yard from Chalk Hill and can also see people when they are moving about with the naked eye and with a field glass you can tell who they are."

Llewellyn informed Fraser that he had sent a Mr. Skidmore over to see his daughter, Mrs. Lew Cowan, to learn Fall's actions that day and the time Fall left Sunol. Later in the night, Llewellyn showed up at Fraser's hotel room to report to him that Skidmore had returned and his daughter told him that Fall did not leave Sunol later than 3:00 or 4:00 p.m., "and if this be the case then he should have driven where he met Mr. Cox in an hour but instead of that he does not reach this part of the road until after 8:30 p.m. . . . ."

As they talked, Llewellyn and Fraser were joined by Thomas Branigan, who lived with Llewellyn. Fraser was informed that a statement of the search party's trip had been typed up by Llewellyn and would be signed by all the posse members. The statement was to accompany Fraser's report, but it has been lost to history.[11] This was most likely the same statement search party member and Lee friend Henry Stoes refused to sign because he did not agree with the majority opinion.[12]

The afternoon brought Fraser's first meeting with Captain Eugene Van Patten. The fifty-six-year-old Van Patten had just returned from a search for the bodies led by Pat Garrett. They had found none, but Van Patten said they found where something had been buried and then dug up and he thought that the bodies had been removed and taken somewhere else by the murderers.[13]

Fraser asked Van Patten if he had heard of the three men who were reported by the mail carrier as watching the road. Van Patten had heard of the men, said they had run them down, and that they were James Gililland, Dan Fitchett, and a man named McDougal, all of whom, according to Van Patten, belonged to the Oliver Lee gang. Van Patten said when he and two other men rode up to them, the three came at them with their rifles ready to use. When they saw Garrett and the seven other men come up over the hill they pulled up. They claimed they were looking for cattle. Fraser observed, "Now to go back a few years, I wish to state that I am informed by Gov. Thornton and others here that about 1882 one Walter Goode [Good] was killed by Oliver Lee, Tom Tucker, Bill Kellum [Kellam], known as Cherokee Bill, and his body was buried in what is known as the White Sands and were watched for a long time in the same manner as these men have been watching the road in the vicinity of Lunas [Luna's] Wells."

Fraser wrote that Llewellyn "is also very well satisfied and so do all the people here with whom I have come in contact seem to be, that the negro barber Ellis knows all about this affair; Van Patten is now working on him through a Mexican woman whom he lays up with."[14]

Llewellyn also told Fraser "that there was nothing in connection with Col. Fountain's domestic affairs to cause him to disappear and that there was never any trouble between his wife and himself. . . . Mrs. Fountain they say is flighty and can give no more information than they have; she blames herself for letting the boy go as the Col. did not want to take him."

Fraser then got his first look at items found at the murder scene when Van Patten showed him the nickel and dime found at Chalk Hill. Fraser observed that the nickel had "stains on it which might have been blood, but they are very dim" and the dime had "the appearance of being powder burned on one side only and is still black." Garrett and Perry came in for the night reporting no trace of the bodies, only terrible weather "on account of the cold wind and sand."

Fraser made some other observations in that day's report. Commenting on the ugly situation he was hearing about, the detective pointed out that he was still undercover to the general public. "So far I have been able to keep under cover as I am supposed to be connected with Fraser & Chalmers, the Mining Machinery Co., and I thought owing to the condition of affairs here and the number of spies on the other side of this case that it would be as well to keep under cover as long as possible."

He added another note on the condition in Las Cruces. "To show how things are being watched by some one, or several every-time [sic] one of the citizens who is interested in this affair leave town on the Tularosa road, they no sooner pass out of town than a shot is fired for each one in the party and the same way when any person or party comes in." The shots were only fired at night. Fires and another signal were supposedly used during the day.[15]

The next day, Fraser finally had a chance to speak to Pat Garrett. The talk was cut short, however, since Garrett was taking the noon train to El Paso. From there, Garrett would go to Santa Fe to meet with Governor Thornton. Fraser decided he couldn't wait, that it was important that he speak with Garrett, and followed him to El Paso. The two, along with Charles Perry, met at Garrett's room in the Lindell Hotel.[16]

Garrett told Fraser that no trace of the bodies had been found. When told of Van Patten's statement about finding where bodies had been dug up and removed, Garrett acted surprised and said, "there was not a word of truth to it." He said no men were watching the road. "Van Patten can not be relied on at all," according to Garrett. They discussed other evidence. Fraser reported that Garrett continued:

> He does not think that negro Ellis the barber at Las Cruces knows a thing about this killing. Fall may know but he don't think he was present at the killing. He thinks there were more than three and certainly not more than five. Joe Morgan may have been in on it and Oliver Lee, Bill McNew, and Jas. R. Gilliland [Gililland] are no doubt the men who held the Col. up near Chalk Hill and the blood found on the road near Chalk Hill is where the Col. was held up and killed, and those bodies will be found somewhere within five miles of where he was killed.
>
> He told me that Jack Tucker was not in on it nor was Tom Tucker, but they belonged to the same outfit. Garrett said it would be utterly impossible for any stranger to approach Oliver Lee or this outfit without getting killed, as they were very suspicious and it would simply mean the death of any man who went in here to operate. The outfit was cold blooded and it would be nothing for them to kill anyone whom they suspected.

Fraser asked Garrett if there was any place they could put a man on, and Garrett responded that "there was only one place and that was to put a good man onto a woman named Richardson at Tularosa or near there." Richardson was "intimate" with Bill McNew "and she no doubt knew a great deal about this gang."

Fraser reported:

Garrett said he did not think it was a good plan for me to go out and interview these people on the Tularosa road as I would get nothing for they had all been talked to and were scared to death of this gang of thieves and murderers. He declared that a trip of this kind would be very dangerous for me to make as Lee and his crowd would not hesitate to kill a man who openly went into that country to investigate this case. From further conversation with Mr. Garrett I saw very plainly that he did not want me to go out and cause a stir by an open investigation. He told me that what he wanted me to do was to try to pull everybody off from the idea that Oliver Lee, Gilliland, and McNew are the men and to stop them from talking so much. He further stated that if he could be made sheriff in place of the present incumbent he would have things where he could start right in on this gang . . .

Fraser made an important observation on the care of the evidence. "I find that various articles that will figure as evidence in this case such as the coins found, also the napkin and piece of boy's shirt waist and other articles have not been kept together, but are scattered all over; some articles in the hands of one and some in others. I would suggest that all the articles pertaining to the case be properly marked for identification by parties who found them and then turned over to one reliable person and locked safely away." The operative's long day ended at 2:20 a.m.[17]

Two days later, Fraser left El Paso and spent most of the day in Las Cruces while Garrett met with the governor in Santa Fe. Fraser learned in a letter from a J. P. Meadows that Meadows had learned where Jack Tucker was the day of the murder and claimed he could not have been involved.

Fraser received another letter, through Llewellyn, "from a Mrs. S. E. Barber, written at White Oaks, N. M. and dated Mar. 6, 1896." Anyone familiar with the Lincoln County War history will know Susan Barber by the name of her late first husband, McSween.

In the letter, Barber wrote that Jack Maxwell claimed to have stopped at Lee's ranch the night Fountain disappeared. She pointed out that Maxwell seemed to have "plenty of money which he claims was left him by a relative who died," but Barber did not believe him and was working on Maxwell to find out what he knew. Barber said that Maxwell told her that he was going to Mexico but did not know where to go as he knew no one down there. She said that he was stopping at Bud Smith's ranch, and added that Smith also claimed to have been at Lee's ranch on the same night that Jack Maxwell was. She said she did not know whether this story was true or not. "It is her opinion that Jack Maxwell is one of the guilty men and that Bud Smith is accessory to the crime."

Of Susan Barber, Fraser noted that she was "a ranch and cattle owner and a pretty bright woman. She is said to have handled her virtue in a rather reckless manner former days, but of late she had joined the church and is now one of the leading members . . ."[18]

In Santa Fe, Garrett and Thornton were differing on the course of action Fraser should take. Thornton disagreed with Garrett about whether Fraser should go out on the road. Thornton wrote to Fraser following his meeting with Pat Garrett. In the March 10 letter, the governor wrote, "I differ with Mr. G. as to the course he is pursuing, and so advised him. I think that you should go upon the ground, examine and talk to every witness, and thoroughly inform yourself of all the different clues, so that you can make up your mind from an inspection of the premises and from known facts as to who the guilty parties are and the best mode of procedure."

Thornton informed Fraser that he was to leave for Washington the next day. He made $300 available for Fraser at the bank and told

Fraser to quit if he used up that amount or finished his work, and when Thornton returned the next man would be put on the case if he was thought to be needed. Thornton added that he asked Pat Garrett to stop off at Socorro the next day to look into a "clue."[19]

The following day Garrett did not go to Socorro as the governor had requested of him, but arrived back in Las Cruces on the 10:05 a.m. train.

Garrett met with Fraser that afternoon and the two talked about Garrett's meeting with Thornton. Fraser reported, "He told me of his talk with the Governor and that he agreed with him about my not making the trip, but later he told me that the Gov. said we could do as we saw fit and thought best, and then Mr. Garrett added that the trip would do no good except to enable me to give them my opinion after going over the ground." It must not have occurred to Garrett that Thornton would write Fraser with his view of the subject. Moments later, Garrett would tell Fraser that the governor thought it best that Fraser remain in Las Cruces "and look after the case and advise them on various points that might come up." Fraser would receive Thornton's letter the next day. Garrett's tendency to withhold information and in some cases lie would strain his relationship with the Pinkerton operative. It was obvious that Garrett did not believe he needed and did not want Fraser's help. Maybe Garrett was worried Fraser would try to collect a portion of the reward, though Garrett should have been aware the Pinkertons forbade their operatives from accepting rewards.

Fraser brought up the statement of Eva Taylor, who claimed to have seen three horsemen Sunday morning at 6:00 a.m. and to have recognized Lee and McNew and thought the third person was a man named Chatfield, but was unsure. Garrett said this was out of the question, that Jack Maxwell was at Lee's Saturday and Sunday and he saw Lee, McNew, and Gililland ride into Lee's ranch Sunday morning at about 9 a.m., "and they were all fagged out and so were the horses."

The two men also discussed Ed Brown and "Slick" Miller, who were involved in an 1894 plot to kill Colonel Fountain. Fraser's first information on Ed Brown had come the previous day when he received a letter in which Brown was mentioned. What information was in the letter Fraser did not report, and the letter has since been lost.[20] Garrett told Fraser, "Ed Brown may have been in this job, and if so, the trail leading through the Pass in the Mountains would account for him as that would be right on his way home and also in the proper direction to dispose of the bodies in the manner planned in 1894 which was to be in the San Andreas Mts." Brown, according to Garrett, was said to have left Socorro a few days before the disappearance of Colonel Fountain and was seen in the Cottonwood Groves near Rincon a day or so after the disappearance.

Fraser finished the day: "I was around through the stores and saloons as is my custom each day, but did not pick up anything new."[21] The next day, Fraser made another observance of Garrett in his report. "This morning I got out my report and then called on Mr. Garrett at his room and had another talk with him; he is a man who says very little, so anything I learn from him is through questions."

Fraser made another note on Lee: "Garrett says Oliver Lee told him when he questioned him that he was home on his ranch on Saturday, Feb. 1st, which, if the statements of Maxwell and Dan Fitchett are true, the latter I understand waited three or four days at Lee's ranch with a bunch of cattle which he was to deliver, but could not do so as Oliver was not home."[22]

In the meantime, Reymond received a victory in the unsettled sheriff's contest, which was in court in Silver City. This was a severe blow that took much of the morale out of the Democrats fighting the case. However, they weren't ready to concede just yet. Ascarate immediately appealed the decision, which kept anything from changing for the moment. Garrett was frustrated as the process dragged out. He felt powerless and didn't want to make any more moves until he was an officer himself.

Meanwhile, Fraser received Thornton's letter of the tenth in that day's mail, then decided to make his trip. When he told Garrett of his decision, Garrett "acted very nicely about it and said I should go out with them which I decided to do on account of their knowledge of the country and of the people that I want to see."[23]

John C. Fraser
(Date and photographer unknown. Courtesy of the Library of Congress, Pinkerton National Detective Agency collection.)

Rio Grande Hotel, circa 1890
(Date and photographer unknown. Courtesy New Mexico State University Library, Archives and Special Collections, Branigan Memorial Library photographs, A76-157/44.)

Las Cruces, circa 1890
(Date and photographer unknown. Courtesy New Mexico State
University Library, Archives and Special Collections, Branigan Memorial
Library photographs, Ms00010053.)

six

Assistance from Fall

On Friday, March 13, Albert Fall called on Pat Garrett in his hotel room. When he stopped by Garrett's room, Fraser must have been surprised to see Fall there. After Fraser and Fall had exchanged a few pleasantries about the weather, Fraser left so Garrett and Fall could continue their conversation.

Fall told Garrett that he wanted him to have a commission as a deputy sheriff, regardless of the outcome of the sheriff's contest. Although an obvious ploy to get on Garrett's good side, as it seemed he would inevitably become sheriff sooner or later, the increasingly frustrated Garrett was glad for whatever help he could get. Fall promised to go to Santa Fe and throw his support behind Garrett.[1]

Garrett was to leave for El Paso later that day. He told Fraser before he left that he hoped to be placed in office before he went out again, so that he would have the power to act if he saw fit. Fraser noted, "This will keep me here until he goes out, for I fail to find anyone who wants to go out with me on this trip alone as driver and guide . . . ."

Fraser also observed Lee that day. "I saw Oliver Lee on the street here to-day, he is not a bad looking man, being a Deputy Sheriff he wore his belt and pistol; he was around Fall's office and Ellis's barber shop."[2] Fraser next wanted to interview Albert Fall. He checked at Fall's office three or four times Saturday morning, but Fall was not in. Fraser then headed to El Paso with Llewellyn and S. B.

Newcomb. There he met Ben Williams for the first time. Williams gave Fraser his thoughts on "the Oliver Lee gang": "Williams is thoroughly satisfied that it was the Oliver Lee gang who did this work and told me that he knew them well, as he has been among them for two years and had to quit them because he would not join them in their murderous work." Williams said he was working to get a case of murder against Lee and others in Texas, and said he would be ready in a few weeks to arrest Oliver Lee, "who comes to El Paso very often to see this woman who runs the furnished rooming house."

Ben Williams had been living in El Paso since being attacked by this "gang headed by A. B. Fall" in Las Cruces. Fraser saw Oliver Lee several times on the streets of El Paso that day, and observed that Lee wore his belt and pistols there, just as he did at Las Cruces.

Fraser stopped at the post office upon his return to Las Cruces Sunday. Waiting for him was a letter from Thornton.[3] Thornton wrote Fraser that he would do what he could to see that no hitch was made in the effort to have Pat Garrett put in as deputy sheriff, and added, "I feel however, that what I do, should be done quietly."

Thornton then expressed his hope that Garrett had told Fraser about an affidavit Garrett obtained from someone who on the night of the murder was supposedly staying at a house near the scene and saw three horsemen, some of the parties suspected, the next morning. Thornton said of Garrett, "He said that he had some hesitancy in telling you because he had promised this party that he would tell no one about it. I told Garrett that you must have this information in order to arrive at a correct solution of the matter."[4] Fraser noted in his report, "I received two letters from Gov. Thornton both dated March 13th, and in one of those he asks me if Mr. Garrett had told me about an affidavit he had from a man who stayed all night at a house near the scene of the murder and who saw men return the following morning, etc. I wish to state that Mr. Garrett has never said one word to me about having received an affidavit from any one, and any information I get from him is mostly obtained by questioning so it can be readily seen that I am working at a great disadvantage."[5]

Accompanying that day's report was a list of items removed from Fountain's buckboard.

1   40-82 Winchester rifle, rear sight taken off and replaced by piece of white metal in slot of same. Front sight small ivory bead, adjustable Lyman sight back of hammer, nose of stock cut out to permit Lyman sight to fold back into stock; one side of stock worn crossways about three inches from butt and, caused by rubbing against foot rail.

1   Celluloid handled dagger and sheath (drawing of same is now in possession of P. F. Garrett)

1   Canteen 9 inches in diameter (mate of which can be seen at Col. Fountain's house)

1   Bridle with blinds (mate can be seen at Fountain's)

1   One inch rope 40 feet long (old)

1   Lap robe, one side black the other red with dogs heads printed in black and two whips crossed behind the dogs' heads.

1   Indian blanket 3 X 5 feet, red, white, blue, green, and yellow in saw teeth design.

1   Quilt.

2   Neck yoke straps.

This list was made up by a Mr. Clawson [Carl Clausen], a son-in-law of Col. Fountain and is supposed to be correct.[6]

On Monday morning, March 16, Fraser prepared to leave for Socorro to investigate Ed Brown's possible connection to the Fountain case. As Fraser readied to depart, Llewellyn asked him if he had seen the letters from Dr. Charles Cruickshank in regard to the Ed Brown matter. This was the first Fraser had heard of any letters on the subject. Llewellyn informed him that they had been turned over to Garrett. When Fraser asked Garrett about the letters, he said he had paid no attention to them. Garrett told the operative that the letters contained the same information that he already had about Ed Brown returning to his ranch a few days after Fountain's disappearance with worn-out horses. The information in the letter came from José Angel Gallegos, who was the man Thornton had instructed Garrett to meet when he came down from Santa Fe on the eleventh. The information came by the letter since Garrett did not stop off at Socorro as instructed.

Fraser finished speaking with Garrett then left for Socorro shortly before noon.[7]

On his way up to Socorro, at Rincon, Fraser was introduced to Judge Gideon D. Bantz. Bantz, who was named to replace Fall when he resigned, was the judge who would decide the sheriff's contest.[8] Fraser, who explained to Bantz the conditions he had found in Las Cruces, said Judge Bantz seemed very interested and asked a lot of questions. Fraser also said of Bantz: "He expressed himself very strongly as being opposed to the manner in which people were being murdered. I had but a few moments before my train pulled out to talk, but from the manner in which Judge Bantz expressed himself I should judge that he would decide in favor of Numa Raymond [Reymond]."[9]

Fraser arrived at Socorro at 5:15 p.m. He went to the court-house to find Elfego Baca, who was the county clerk and one of the men whom Thornton had instructed Fraser to see. Fraser learned that Elfego Baca and Librado C. de Baca were out in the country on some political business. Fraser left word where he could be found and at 7 p.m. Librado C. de Baca came to his hotel.

De Baca informed Fraser that Baca had gone to San Marcial the previous day and saw José Angel Gallegos, with whom he was well acquainted. Baca learned from him that a man who worked for Ed Brown and who owned a ranch close to Brown's could give the day and date that Brown, Green Scott, and another man left and returned and what was said before and after their return. Baca had told de Baca that the man who worked for Brown could give the name of the third man as well, and tell what horses they rode in on. Fraser reported that one of the three claimed he was at court in Lincoln but no one saw him there. The men claimed they were going to get some cattle and drive them in, but they brought no cattle. "Gallegos told Mr. Baca that he was positive that these men killed Col. Fountain, but this was simply his own opinion." Baca also claimed that he overheard Green Scott say he was "glad that son of a bitch Col. Fountain was dead."[10]

Librado C. de Baca left and returned with the thirty-one-year-old former sheriff, Elfego Baca.[11] Baca and Fraser were introduced and Baca gave Fraser the same evidence, "almost word for word" that de Baca had given. Then Baca took the conversation on an unexpected turn, as Fraser reported:

> he informed me rather bluntly that he did not think he should be called upon to do this for nothing and it was only a question of money with him. I explained the condition of affairs and mentioned the reward; he said he knew all about that, but Pat Garrett had been hired and others, and he himself had a good record as sheriff of this county. He went on to tell of the different desperate men whom he had captured, and I saw at once that he seemed to think he should have been called upon to act. He told me that I could tell Pat Garrett just how he felt about it. He went on to say that if he was in a position to go to this Mexican and say, "Here is a certain sum of money," and place the sum in his hand, "now tell me what you

know, I would get the whole thing." Mr. Baca said there was no doubt about these being the men, still I found from our conversation that this was simply his own idea from what little he knew through Gallegos. I went over [to] town and treated them to cigars and drinks . . . .[12]

Back in Las Cruces on Tuesday, Fraser and Garrett decided they would leave for their trip that Thursday. Fraser and Llewellyn walked through Las Cruces that evening. There had been a terrible dust storm that day and, as a result, few people were out. After the stores had closed, Fraser and Llewellyn called on John Riley, a former cattleman in New Mexico who had moved away "on account of this lawless gang." During their conversation, Fraser was told that Ed Brown had been indicted and sent to jail several times by Fountain.[13]

The next morning, Fraser took the statement of William Webb Cox, whose father was killed in Texas's Sutton-Taylor feud.[14] W. W. Cox recalled meeting both Fall and Joe Morgan on the road from Las Cruces, but was unsure of the times. (Llewellyn previously had said that Cox told him he met Fall at 8:30 p.m.) Cox ended his statement with concern for the growing violence in the area. "I came from a country where men kill each other, but not children."[15]

Fraser began the afternoon walking the street with Garrett. Fraser mentioned to Garrett that he would like to speak with Fall and Lee before he went out on the road. It was at this time that they ran into Bascom, whose first name was possibly Fred, who was a member of one of the initial searching parties. Fraser was introduced to Bascom. While Fraser and Bascom spoke, Garrett excused himself and walked down the street toward Fall's office. Fraser could see Garrett talking to someone in front of Bull's store. Garrett soon returned and told Fraser that Fall would see him in his office and that at the request of Garrett he had sent for Oliver Lee to come. This was not what Fraser had planned. "I told Mr. Garrett that this was a mistake as I did not want to talk to these men together, but separately, but it was too late to find fault." At least Garrett was trying to be more helpful than when they first met.

When Fraser arrived at Fall's office, he observed quite a crowd in the rear room. He did not recognize any of them except attorney Harvey Fergusson and Fall, although he admittedly did not get a good look into the room. He figured they were discussing the sheriff's contest. Fall brought a lamp into the front office, where he and Fraser could talk and be alone. Fraser immediately explained Garrett's mistake, as he was anxious to get through with Fall before Lee arrived. Fraser reported:

> Fall's talk to me was not in the form of a statement, but a general talk as I had come to him to get what information I could, the same as I would go to any citizen. After explaining my position in the matter and impressing on him the fact of this being an impartial investigation in which politics or reward cut no figure. Judge Fall expressed himself as being well pleased to have some one come in here who would make an investigation of this kind; he then turned loose by first saying that he would state his position in this case; he did not like Col. Fountain any more than he did a snake . . . .

Fall said he had had dealings with Fountain and "the man was not straight and he would mould witnesses and testimony to suit his case." Once Fall got started down this path, he did not let up. Fall said of Fountain,

He is a man who has killed several men and I will cite you one case to show you what kind of man he was. He was conveying a prisoner for horse stealing over a line of railroad down here some years ago and at the time his son, Albert, was a Colonel in the Militia down here. The prisoner was said to have tried to escape and was shot dead by Colonel Fountain as he got off the train. Fountain said he was 90 steps from the car when he shot and killed him, but the truth of this statement was that Colonel Fountain, when they came in sight of the camp fires of the militia, told the prisoner that the fires belonged to the militia and that it was their intention to take him from the train and hang him and he advised him to drop off the train when it slowed up and get away and that he was his friend and would assist him to do this and did get the conductor of the train to slow up and the prisoner, who still wore handcuffs, dropped off the front platform and Colonel Fountain stood on the steps of the rear platform and shot him dead as he came up to him on the road where he had dropped off. The body was powder burned so he could not have shot him at ninety steps away as he stated. Now this is only one of many cases in which this man has done dirty work.[16]

One wonders how Fall knew what was said or why Fall felt the need to slander Fountain. Was he attempting to help Lee's defense by justifying the killing? He'd go on to make more such attacks, which were not very believable and could not be corroborated, casting doubt on everything Fall said.

It was at this point in their conversation that Oliver Lee arrived. Fall explained Fraser's error to him and then resumed with his thoughts on Fountain. He told the Pinkerton operative that one time Fountain came to him and offered him $1,000 to assist him on a case, but Fall said that he refused on account of manufactured evidence. Fall did not mention what the case was.

Fall went on to say "that Jack Fountain had made some ugly talk about him and told on the street that the murder of his father was put up in his office and that he was at the head of a gang of murders and thieves."[17] It does appear to be true that Jack Fountain said all of these things. He strongly believed that Fall was behind the murder of his father and brother. Jack's brother Albert, on the other hand, was convinced, ever since Fall had him to his office for a meeting, that Fall had nothing to do with the disappearance.[18]

Fall continued, "Now, I want to say to you that I believe Judge Fountain is dead. At first I thought he might have left and would turn up in Cuba as he was a Spanish scholar, and as he was inclined to be sensational, this would just suit him."

Fraser asked Fall if he thought Fountain would take his son with him, providing he had done anything like that. Fall replied that he may have had reasons for taking the boy as he was very much attached to the little fellow and there was a rumor. But before going any further, Fall "stopped and said that it was only a rumor and if advanced by him would be regarded as some plan to revert attention or a trick of his to lead the officers off the right track." Fraser asked him to go ahead and he readily did so by saying it was rumored that Mrs. Fountain had caught the colonel in a compromising position with his own daughter just before he went away. Fall said he could not tell what truth there was in this, as it might be the same as hundreds of other rumors, but said, "I got it from a reliable citizen who got it from some one else."

"Why one of these men who has helped drag this thing into politics claims that the tracks of my buckboard were traced from Sunol to the Chalk Hill where Colonel Fountain was killed, and this man was none other then Major Llewellyn and I am only waiting a chance to tell him what I think about this kind of work."

Fraser assured Fall that he had never heard anything of the kind. Fall responded that he believed that, for they knew if Fraser was told anything of the kind he would investigate and "explode their story." Fall "was pretty hot when he was telling this." Fall said that he had not cut across from Sunol to "any of those roads" since the previous April. Fraser reported, "The Judge then said there were plenty of chances for people to kill Fountain and get into Old Mexico and there were any number of cattle thieves and desperadoes who knew this road, and Col. Fountain had prosecuted a great many people and had used manufactured evidence to convict, still he had convicted very few men; now some of these men may have run across him by chance and killed him."

Fall said, "A man could hide behind a soap weed and catch him where he was caught." Fall continued,

> Now they say that Fountain was a great prosecutor, but I want to tell you that he has convicted only Slick Miller, Davis, and one or two others and that was done on confessions made by some of the gang with whom they have been working; and I want to say further that as a prosecutor and a lawyer no one had anything to fear as he had no standing before any jury and could not make a conviction in Doña Ana County. Now if there are any questions you think of I want you to ask them. If the papers and people had not attacked me as they did, I should have been ready and willing to help run this down. Why Judge McFie of this very place went to my old law partner A. W. Hawkins in El Paso and asked him to get me to assist in running this thing down and Mr. Hawkins went for McFie and told him flat

footed that he had heard him curse and damn me for my connection with the gang of thieves as he termed Mr. Lee, Mr. McNew, Jack Tucker, James Gilliland [sic], Carr and others, all of whom have been dragged into this thing.

Fall laughed and while looking at Lee said, "Poor Jack Tucker, he says he can prove where he was, and he was chopping wood for his wife 70 miles from there." Turning back to Fraser, Fall continued,

Well Mr. Hawkins told Judge McFie to come to me himself and ask me like a man to do so and so and he would find I would do it, and so I would, but the condition of affairs before you came here was something terrible and no one could tell what might happen any minute. The Republican paper here came out and declared that the Democrats killed Fountain. I tell you sir, it was something awful. Yes, things have quieted down since you came and I am glad you outsiders such as Mr. Garrett, Mr. Perry, and yourself have taken hold of this case, for there was no telling what some of these fellows might not try to do.

Lee chimed in to agree with Fall on this point. Fraser noted that "Both these men occupied positions where they could watch each other and Lee kept his eyes on the Judge during the entire conversation." Fall asked Fraser if he had heard that there had been warrants sworn out for Oliver Lee. Fraser said he had heard something about them. Fall said, "Well, Major Llewellyn is the man who wrote the names in these warrants." In reality, there were no warrants out for anyone with regards to the Fountain case at this time.

Fraser asked Fall if he could tell him when he first heard of the disappearance of Colonel Fountain. Fall said he thought it was on the following Monday when he was on his way to El Paso. Fraser then asked if he would explain where he was on the Saturday of the disappearance. At this question, both Fall and Lee burst out laughing and Lee winked at Fall. Fraser told Lee "that he need not laugh as [he] would soon reach him; this caused another laugh as [Fraser] had made this remark in a joking sort of way."

Fall stated that on the day of the disappearance he was at his gold property at Sunol. Fraser asked him if he went out that Friday, and he replied, "No sir, I did not, I was there several days but I can't say just when I did go out as I was making so many trips back and forth from the mine." Fall did remember that District Attorney Young arrived at his place and wanted Fall to go in with him to check out some claims he was interested in. Fall asked him to wait as he was waiting for a Mr. O'Neill to arrive. O'Neill did not arrive and Young left the next morning. Fall continued,

> a short time after him came my brother-in-law, Joe Morgan, who had been out to look at some mining property and was on his way home and arrived in Las Cruces at 3 p.m.; this he can prove by a number of people here. In the afternoon, O'Neill came in and we fixed up our business, which was a mining deal for C. B. Eddy of El Paso and at something near 4 p.m. I hitched up my team of ponies and started for town but had gotten only a few yards from the house when one of them balked and I could do nothing with them, so unhitched and went back and roped my team of mules and at 4 p.m. left for town. I know the time because I looked at my watch as I started. I arrived at Las Cruces at 8 p.m.

Fall laughed: "No, I did not look at my watch on my arrival but I know the time because I went home and ate my supper and we have a clock. No, I met no one on the road that I remember unless it was a Mexican. I did not stop to speak to anyone."[19] Fall's statement that he did not meet anyone on the road conflicts with Cox's statement, but Fall would correct himself in a later meeting with Fraser.[20]

Finished with Fall, Fraser turned his attention to Oliver Lee. He began to ask him what he knew about the matter when Fall interrupted and said he would like to explain Lee's position in this case. He said that Lee had been accused of being connected with the disappearance of Colonel Fountain and as Lee's attorney and friend he had advised him not to tell anyone where he was on that day or any other day, but when the time came Fall had the papers and witnesses to prove where Oliver Lee was. He added, while pointing with his right hand toward Lee, "I have letters that you know nothing about." Lee took Fall's advice and said nothing of his whereabouts.

Fraser reported:

> Fall said he had told me what he would not tell
> another damn man in the town and that was where
> he spent his time on Saturday. I then had some talk
> with Oliver Lee but learned nothing. I noticed that
> Lee always watched Judge Fall and the Judge kept
> looking at him all the time; at one time he started
> to tell something, but Fall shook his head and Lee,
> who was looking straight at him stopped short and
> began talking about something else.

Fall, becoming part of the conversation again, said he didn't think that Governor Thornton "had acted right in this matter" and was to blame for "swinging this affair into politics."

Fall told Fraser that two more men, Frank Hill and Hiram Yost, were said to have been connected with the killing. He told Fraser that if he wanted any information in regard to them that he should come to Fall before he left and Fall would tell him where they were and show him that they could not have been involved. Fraser assured Fall that he had never heard these names mentioned. Later Fraser would learn that Garrett had just received information that Yost and Hill may have been connected with the case.

With the interview done, Fraser invited Fall and Lee to the corner saloon. Fraser noted, "Lee does not smoke or drink." While there, one of the topics they discussed was the sheriff's contest. Both Lee and Fall said Judge Bantz would decide in favor of Numa Reymond, and Lee added that he would be defeated in the upper court on appeal. Fall left and returned to his office where people were still waiting for him. Fraser "discontinued at 1:05 a.m."[21]

Albert Fall (Date and photographer unknown. Courtesy New Mexico State University Library, Archives and Special Collections, Herman Weisner papers, Ms0249.)

seven

Decision in the Sheriff's Contest

A decision in the sheriff's contest came down on March 19. Judge Bantz ruled in favor of Numa Reymond and instructed him to take office the next morning. Unfortunately, it did not appear to be a given that Garrett would be made chief deputy, and subsequently sheriff. Reymond told Garrett that he had made several promises to Oscar Lohman and others for positions on his staff and was not inclined to turn the office over to him. Reymond offered to make Garrett a deputy sheriff and to assist him all he could in the Fountain case. Garrett did not want to listen to this and walked out.

This situation obviously frustrated Fraser as well, who was eager to see this settled so that Garrett could concentrate on the Fountain case and accompany him on his trip of the sites. Fraser wrote, "I spent most of the day and evening trying to get this matter straightened out so that I would meet with no further delay, but when I discontinued matters were even worse than in the morning." Llewellyn told Fraser that he and John Riley would go see Reymond and Lohman and try to get the matter straightened out, but the day ended without resolution.[1]

While all of this was going on, there were some new developments in the case. Sheriff Perry of Roswell had left to get warrants for the arrest of James Gililland on a charge of cattle theft and the intention was to place him in jail until he talked. Chaves County Deputy Sheriff Les Dow was to make the arrest. Fraser noted, "This man Gilliland [*sic*] is said to be weak and is thought to be a good man to work on."

Albert Christy told Fraser and Garrett a story he was told by a man named Santa Rosa Rico. Rico had said that his brother-in-law Pedro Serna and District Attorney Young stopped at Fall's Sunol ranch on Friday, January 31, and that no one was home. Fall and Joe Morgan arrived there at about 10:00 that night. They talked with Young, and Serna said he heard them cursing someone and heard Colonel Fountain's name mentioned.

Fraser was told another story from Fall's Sunol property, which was the first real information he received about Frank Hill and Hiram Yost. John Riley informed him that one Charles Jones had told his brother-in-law Russell Walters that Hiram Yost and Frank Hill were at Sunol Gold Camp on Thursday, January 30. Fraser noted, "Hiram Yost is a first cousin to Tom and Jack Tucker and Frank Hill is a nephew to Frank Graham who was mixed up in the Pleasant Valley Arizona war against the Tewksbury boys."[2]

The next day Fraser ran into Fall on the streets of Las Cruces and asked Fall to walk down the street with him. Fraser asked if Oliver Lee had ever made a statement to anyone regarding his whereabouts at the time of the disappearance. Fall stated that he did not, contradicting Garrett's claim that Lee told him he was at his ranch at the time. When Fall and Fraser stopped opposite Max Shutz's store, Fraser asked him if he did not think it was a mistake not to allow Oliver Lee to make a statement explaining where he was at the time of the disappearance. "Fall replied very promptly that he did not think it was a mistake and that he had carefully considered the matter before advising him to say nothing to anyone." Fraser "asked him if in the face of all the talk about this case he did not think it was poor judgment for him not to make a statement and again he said no." Fall then told Fraser "how this affair was all politics and that certain people only wanted a chance to kill Oliver Lee . . . ." He said that Llewellyn "and other Republicans had placed armed men in the street on election day three years ago," and told "how a man had been brought in from Nebraska to kill him (Fall) and through all this Oliver Lee was the only man whom he could call on and trust . . . ." He added that "Lee had never committed a crime since he had been in this country." Fraser reported, "I broke in to say that Lee was not accused of any connection in this case and for this reason I thought he should make a statement. I further stated that I had noticed how bad it looked for him not to make a statement when I came to write up my report."[3] Fall's response is not reported.

It was here that Fall corrected his earlier statement about the night of the murder, stating that he had in fact met someone, Mr. Cox and his brother, on the road from Sunol to Las Cruces. After a little further conversation, Fall had to leave as he was informed that someone wanted to speak with him on the telephone.

The matter of the sheriff's contest was still being discussed, but even though Garrett was getting closer to becoming sheriff, nothing was final and even if he was given charge of the office, he informed Fraser he would not be able to leave on their trip for two or three days. Not being able to wait that long, Fraser made arrangements with Llewellyn to used his team of mules and buggy and for his son Morgan to accompany Fraser on the trip as a guide. Fraser and Morgan Llewellyn left at 4:10 that afternoon.[4]

During Fraser's trip, the problems surrounding the sheriff's office were worked out and Garrett was made chief deputy on the twenty-second and then sheriff when Reymond resigned several weeks later. It is not known what was said in the meeting with Numa Reymond and Oscar Lohman, but rumor had it that Las Cruces businessmen raised $1,000 and paid the two.[5]

John Fraser and Morgan Llewellyn spent their first night on the slopes of the Organ Mountains at the Bennett and Stevenson Mine. Leaving there the next morning, they stopped at Parker's Well, went on to Chalk Hill, and then to Luna's Well. Fraser conducted interviews at each stop. At Luna's Well Fraser received second-hand information about someone seeing, on the day Colonel Fountain passed through, "two men about a quarter of a mile from the ranch off the road east of the main road; but he could not tell who they were, but one rode a gray horse and one a bay [reddish brown] horse and both wore white hats."

Fraser and Morgan moved on and spent the night at Pellman's Well. F. W. Pellman told Fraser that he saw Colonel Fountain and Henry at his place on February 1. They were there from noon until about 2:00 p.m. Fountain fed and watered his horses, and he carried a lunch that he and Henry ate near Pellman's corral. Pellman, who said he had known Fountain for fifteen years, told Fraser that the two had a good deal of talk about politics, but Fountain never said a word about anybody following him nor did he speak of indictments or court matters. Pellman did not see anyone else pass by his home during that time.

John Meadows and E. E. Banner, for whom Fraser left a note at Luna's Well, came up to Pellman's to speak with Fraser. Meadows told Fraser that he would not find Jack Maxwell "as he was keeping shadowed." He said that McNew and Gililland were hiding out in the Sacramento Mountains and "Joe Morgan was over at Tularosa drunk." Fraser reported, "Mr. Banner informed me that they had ascertained positively where Jack Tucker was on that day and that he was not in this affair as an actual participant, still he may have taken a part in it by watching the Col. while he was going through from Lincoln and posted some other members of the gang."[6] He would have this confirmed by another man while in Tularosa.[7]

Fraser arrived at Tularosa before noon the next day and had an amusing interaction with H. K. Parker and his wife. Mrs. Parker gave her statement first, as Fraser was unable to find H. K. Parker, with whom he really wanted to speak. Mrs. Parker told Fraser, "My husband H. K. Parker and C. R. Scott went over the road after Colonel Fountain. They left Tularosa on Friday afternoon. Both were drunk at the time they left and they carried liquor with them. They camped about ten miles from Tularosa in the vicinity of the lost river." She said they had a load of oats they left at Pellman's, and from there they went to El Paso. She was certain her husband did not see Colonel Fountain, any stranger, or any men on horseback or he would have told her, for the Fountain affair had been discussed "a great deal" in town. She thought he camped beyond Chalk Hill on Saturday night, but was unsure. As to the current whereabouts of her husband, Mrs. Parker said, "I don't know where you can find him now unless he is in the Bank saloon. He is most likely drunk as he has not come home to his dinner, but I received word a little while ago that he was going to Three Rivers."

Fraser tracked down H. K. Parker and wrote of the meeting, "Late in the afternoon I met H. K. Parker, but he was so drunk that I could get no intelligent statement from him, the man appeared to me to be on the verge of delirium tremens; I was in hopes I could get him home and after a sleep get a statement from him, but I found this was out of the question and had to leave him without obtaining any information, except that he verified in main the statement made by his wife."[8]

Fraser conducted numerous interviews in Tularosa. In the afternoon, Judge William D. Bailey sought out Fraser to inform him of what he knew. He told Fraser that "he saw Col. Fountain on Friday, January 31st, at about noon in front of Adam J. Dieter's store, and after the Col. had driven away toward La Luz he saw Jack Tucker peeping around in the direction where the Col. drove out to reach the road to La Luz, and that he afterwards saw Jack Tucker riding a sorrel [yellowish or reddish brown] horse which seemed much worn up the road which passes Mr. Shield's [Shields'] and Mrs. McDonald's . . . ." Bailey stated that Tucker acted as though he wanted to avoid being seen. Bailey called "Hello" to Tucker as he passed and he replied. Bailey said that if Jack Tucker was going home he should have taken the same road that Fountain took to La

Luz, "but he seemed to be taking the other road or lane which lies beyond Mr. Shield's house and from which point he might be able to see Col. Fountain for some distance . . . ."[9]

When Fraser spoke with Adam Dieter, Dieter confirmed seeing Jack Tucker but had not paid much attention to him and did not notice his behavior. Dieter said that he gave Fountain forty pounds of oats for his horses. Fraser also met with Shields, who said he spoke to Fountain before he left. Bailey, Dieter, and Shields all said that Fountain had never mentioned being followed.

Earlier that day Fraser had been told of one man, Bernadillo Gomez, who had told another man that he could find the bodies of Fountain and his son, with the exception of one arm. Gomez was brought to town that evening. He told Fraser that he and another man worked to get information from Antonio Rey, who at first would not talk. Rey finally told them that they would find the Fountain bodies in the direction of the San Nicolas Pass in the Sand Hills. The bodies were in a wagon sheet and one arm was gone. He also told the story of a man who went to the top of Rey's house about the time that Fountain passed over the road on his way to Lincoln. Rey claimed not to know the name. The man was said to have gone on the roof many times, apparently watching for someone. He later was said to have stopped at a house at Luna's Well the day before the disappearance.

Fraser and Morgan went to La Luz that evening. In La Luz, Fraser learned from David Sutherland that a woman had seen two armed, red-faced, bearded men with packs and noted, "Bill Carr at that time wore a full beard and was seen in town Friday evening. . . ."[10]

Heading back the next day, the two stopped at Pellman's again and then went on to Luna's Well, where Fraser again interviewed Antonio Rey. He told Rey of the story he had heard, about Rey being able to find the bodies, without mentioning his sources. Rey denied the story, and claimed that what he had said was that he told a party to search in the vicinity of San Nicolas Pass. He also stated that he had told a good many stories to people who had come by just to get rid of them. He denied the story of a man on his roof twenty days before Fountain's disappearance, but did admit that Joe Morgan had at one time been on his roof looking around, though that was long before Colonel Fountain's trip to Lincoln. Rey claimed not to know what Morgan was looking for. Of the interviews of Rey, his wife, and of Santos Alvarado, Fraser noted, "It is hard to tell whether these people are telling the truth, but I am inclined to think that Antonio Rey knows nothing more than what he has already told."

While at Parker's Well that evening, Fraser asked Charles Jones about the story that Yost and Hill were at Sunol around the time Fountain was killed. Jones said he saw Yost but never saw Frank Hill there.[11]

John Fraser and Morgan Llewellyn arrived back at Las Cruces at about 1 p.m. the next day. Fraser reported:

> I saw Mr. Garrett and Mr. Perry in Garrett's room and was told by Garrett that Perry had not succeeded in getting the warrants for Gilliland [Fraser consistently misspells Gililland's name] which he had expected; however, Garrett's manner in reply to my questions led me to believe that Garrett was perhaps holding back information from me; he did not seem to care to talk on the subject and I did not press him. Garrett and Perry were preparing to leave town to make a search for the bodies. I gave Garrett all the information that I had and was surprised on several occasions while reading my notes to him to have Mr. Perry say that there was nothing in this or that statement as he had or they had investigated these points before. It seemed very strange to me if

these points were investigated that Mr. Garrett and Mr. Perry did not give me the result of their investigation as I was there to assist them in every possible way that I could. Mr. Garrett asked me while reading my statement in reference to H. K. Parker bringing a load of oats to Pellman's whether or not I had found out what kind of oats these were. I then learned for the first time that the supposed assassins fed their horses oats where the camp fire was found beyond Col. Fountain's buck board, the oats fed were unthrashed. Now this seems to have been a very important point and I was surprised that I had never been told of it before as I was in a position to make a thorough investigation in reference to these oats had I known anything about it. . . . I found in my conversation with Garrett that he thought that Parker and Scott may have encountered the assassins of Col. Fountain, as they were on the road behind the Col. and that they may have supplied the oats which the assassins fed their horses; this, however, I think hardly probable, as Col. Fountain was at least two hours ahead of Parker and Scott and the men who were keeping track of Col. Fountain were probably ahead of him . . . .

His work done, it was now time for Fraser to conclude his part of the case. He had a long talk with Judge S. B. Newcomb and also spoke with Llewellyn. Fraser said, "These people seemed very much disappointed and surprised at my withdrawing from the case, and they talked as though they were going to take steps to have me return and handle this case."[12]

eight

Exit John Fraser

Now that John Fraser had completed his investigation, he was to be, as planned, taken off the case and a new operative brought in to investigate.[1]

So on Wednesday, March 25, 1896, Fraser left Las Cruces by train and headed for Denver, but his investigation didn't stop. On the train, he ran into Librado C. de Baca and Elfego Baca. De Baca, the man who told Fraser about Ed Brown, Green Scott, and an unidentified man, added to his story. He told Fraser of a statement made to him by one Alexander Garcia, who said "that Ed Brown, Green Scott and the third man whose name he did not know, but whom they called Gene, had left Brown's ranch on Jan. 29th, and returned to Brown's ranch three or four days afterwards, that they afterwards had told that they had only gone as far as Tularosa, that one rode a gray horse, one a sorrel and the other a buck skin [brown with black points]."[2] Back on March 6, Saturnino Barela stated of the men he saw trailing Fountain; "one rode a white horse and the others dark horses . . . ."[3] De Baca continued, offering his opinion that the three men "acted in a very suspicious manner after their return, keeping close to the ranch and evidently always on the lookout for some one."[4] Fraser wrote in regards to Baca and a conversation he had with current Sheriff Numa Reymond, who also happened to be on the train, "After leaving San Marcial I learned from Numa Raymond [Reymond] that Elfego Baca had requested him to put up money so that he might carry on this work on the Ed Brown end of the case. Mr. Raymond consulted with me in regard to this and I advised him not to put up anything at all for I don't think it would be proper or beneficial to the case to give Elfego money to place in the hands of this Mexican to tell something that I don't believe he really knows . . . ."[5]

The next day on the train Fraser, after talking to John Riley at La Junta, stated that Riley and other cattlemen had been talking it over and that they were quite determined that he should return to Las Cruces and continue on the case. "I told Mr. Riley how I had been handicapped in my investigation owing to the fact that information was held back from me by parties interested in the case, and the only way for me to do if I returned on this matter again would be to take one of my own men with me who I could send out to investigate points under our own methods . . . ." Fraser ended his final report in the Fountain case, "I arrived in Denver at 5:15 p.m. reported at the Agency and discontinued."[6]

That same day Pat Garrett presented a contract to Jack Maxwell, offering Maxwell a share of the reward money for his testimony that Lee, Gililland, and McNew were not at Lee's Dog Canyon ranch the night of the Fountain murder, but returned the next day on well-ridden horses. The contract read:

> Tularosa, N. M., March 26, 1896.
> This is to certify that we, the undersigned, agree to pay John Maxwell two thousand dollars ($2000) in case he gives us information that will lead to the arrest and conviction of murderers of Col. A. J. Fountain and son, the said $2000 to be due as soon as the conviction is had.
> (Signed)
> P. F. Garrett, C. C. Perry[7]

Just over a week later, Fraser received a letter from Governor Thornton informing him of the governor's return to Santa Fe. Thornton asked Fraser for the full report of his work and the bill, and left the door open for Fraser's return if his work was not complete.[8]

That same day in Denver, Fraser wrote to Thornton with his conclusions and suggestions of how to proceed. The letter was accompanied by his reports.

Fraser wrote, "You will see from my reports that it has been utterly impossible for me to complete this investigation in anything like a satisfactory manner, owing to the limited time. You will also note that it was impossible for me to get out on the road to Tularosa and La Luz sooner, owing to the wrangle between Numa Raymond and Oscar Loman [Lohman], as the latter insisted on having charge of the Sheriff's office which Mr. Garrett would not listen to." Fraser pointed out that because of this he was "compelled to leave Las Cruces with the son of Major Lewellyn [Llewellyn]" as his interpreter and only had limited for the trip. Fraser continued:

> I feel that this investigation should be continued, and I would suggest that if this matter is taken up again that we be allowed to send one of our men who is a thorough plainsman and an A 1 investigator, to continue this work. Investigations should be made at Engle, Silver City, also investigations that will undoubtedly come up at such points as El Paso, Socorro, San Marcial, and other points over as far as Lincoln and White Oaks, using a saddle horse for this purpose. I think this should be done, as I find that all previous investigations so far have amounted to nothing and has been done in a slip shod manner . . . . in the meantime let Mr. Garrett and Perry continue their search for the bodies of Col. Fountain and his son. I feel satisfied that a good man could

pick up a good deal of information around the country that I have spoken of. You will understand of course that it is impossible for any man to go in there and work secretly on Oliver Lee or any of this gang, but what we do want to get is the statements of these people in full to be used in every case provided arrests are made in the near future. I feel satisfied that this entire matter will come home to Oliver Lee, and that Bill McNew, Jack Tucker, Bill Carr, and others are implicated in this matter. I am thoroughly satisfied that Judge Fall was not at Chalk Hill, but I am not satisfied that he was not a party to the conspiracy. There is certainly a master hand in this whole affair, and the great legal point would be the proper disposition [or] disposal of these bodies so that they could [not] be found. There was nothing to prevent Judge Fall from being able to see what was going on, provided he used a pair of field glasses while at Sunol, for with the naked eye from Chalk Hill you can see Sunol and if Judge Fall was a party to this conspiracy there is nothing to have prevented him from knowing whether or not the plan had been carried out by the other people at Chalk Hill.

Fraser's note on the lack of bodies becoming a legal point would in fact turn out to be an important issue.

I consider the statement of Slick Miller very important in this case. In your last letter to me at Las Cruces you desire to know if I had seen the affidavit which Mr. Garrett had in his possession from some one whose name you did not mention; I wish to

state that Mr. Garrett has positively denied to my
[me] taking any affidavits or receiving any. I did not
let him know that I had received this information
from you, but managed to ask him if any affidavits
had been taken and he stated positively that none
had been taken so far. You can see how I have been
handicapped in this matter and any information I
have gotten from Garrett I have been compelled
to draw out of him by asking questions direct after
having received intimations of what he possessed.
I believe he is thoroughly honest in his intentions,
but may be a little careless and not consider certain
points of much importance. I find that he regards
Mr. Perry as quite a Detective and takes his word
and advice for the truth or falsity of statements
and rumors which come to them. I found that Mr.
Perry treated my investigation at Tularosa and La
Luz in a very light manner and it was he who told
me while I was reading my notes to Garrett that
they had looked these matters up themselves. Now
if our man continues on this work it will not do to
incur the enmity of Garrett, Perry, or any of their
men. I have been very careful not to let them know
that I am aware of their having held information
back from me and at the present time we are the
very best of friends. I simply write this for your
own knowledge, so that you will know exactly how
things are going.

Fraser said that if this plan met with the governor's approval, he
had an operative ready to send out and added, "I would be pleased
to take this work up myself in person were it not for the fact that I
expect to leave for England to-night on an important matter."[9]

80 — Murder on the White Sands

On April 6, Fraser sent Thornton the bill for $299.10. He also informed Thornton that his trip to England was now off and offered, if Thornton thought it necessary, to make a further investigation after the new operative went over the ground.[10]

In a letter that began as if addressed to Fraser, Thornton wrote on April 7 to the head of Pinkerton's Denver office, James McParland, concerning Fraser's reports. He started:

> I think that you are a little mistaken as to Garrett. I told you Garrett had an affidavit from some one who saw the horsemen ride along the road the day the Fountain was killed. . . . I have since seen Garrett and find out that this story, like many others concerning the murder, proved to be a hoax.

Thornton wanted the Pinkertons to continue on the case and was "particularly anxious to have the Ed Brown and Yost clue run down." Thornton believed they knew who the murderers were. He wrote, "As to Garrett and Perry not giving Mr. F. a great deal of information, I do not think it is because they do not want his assistance or help, but because they do not realize the importance of these things. I tried to get Pat to look into the matter of the oats, because of the peculiarity of their being green, and not in a condition to feed to horses and because they might have been traced to whom they were purchased from, but he did not seem to think it amounted to anything."[11]

Fraser wrote on April 11 to respond to Thornton's letter. He informed Thornton that he had sent out operative W. B. Sayers to take up the investigation and addressed his issues with Garrett and Perry. "You may be correct in regard to Mr. Perry and Mr. Garrett, I have every confidence in both of these men and believe they are good officers, but you will admit that they are very careless about giving any information that they may possess. Had they been as frank with me as I was with them they would have saved me a great deal of trouble and I would have been able to have made a more thorough investigation between Las Cruces and Tularosa than I did."[12]

nine

William B. Sayers

Pinkerton operative William B. Sayers then took over the investigation, arriving in Santa Fe in the afternoon on Wednesday, April 15, 1896.[1] When Sayers reached the governor's office the next morning, he found the governor was out of town and he was asked to remain in town till his return. Miss Crane, the governor's stenographer, informed Sayers that there was a letter missing from the governor's table that had been written to him by Fraser. Sayers wrote to McParland asking that a copy of the letter be sent to Thornton so he could see what if any information an outside party could gain from it.[2]

Crane also pointed out Tom Tucker, a Santa Fe deputy sheriff closely associated with Oliver Lee, to Sayers. Sayers watched him and hoped for a chance to speak with him, but it never came.[3] Could Tucker have been responsible for the theft of the letter from the governor's office?

While in Santa Fe, Sayers made plans to interview Ely "Slick" Miller, the twenty-five-year-old who was serving his ten-year prison sentence courtesy of A. J. Fountain.[4] The following morning, after getting a rig at the livery stable, Sayers drove out to the penitentiary and met Colonel Bergamer, who ran the prison, in his office. Upon learning that Sayers planned to be in town through the next day, Bergamer said he thought it was best that he talk with Miller first and then have Sayers question him. Sayers reported, "I did not like this as I would rather see the man myself and have an opportunity to visit him a second time if necessary, but I found the old Col. a most peculiar man and soon saw it was useless to crowd him in any way; he has his own systems of handling his convicts and to urge him to do differently would not do." Bergamer showed Sayers through the penitentiary and pointed out Miller. Bergamer "said that from conversation he had had with the man he was convinced that his story could be depended upon and that he would tell all he knew." Miller had said that he believed he could locate the bodies of Colonel Fountain and his son. Bergamer was of the opinion that they could get some information of value from Miller and said he would talk to him that evening and arrange for Sayers to meet him the next day. Sayers, who wanted to meet Miller earlier, said, "I saw that the Col. was determined on this point so I did not try to force the matter, believing that Col. Bergamer was acting as he considered best and that he was anxious and willing to assist in every way possible to bring to justice Col. Fountain's murderers."

Sayers again noticed Tom Tucker around town that evening, but had no chance to speak to him as Tucker appeared to be busy with the sheriff at the courthouse. Sayers noted, "I noticed Tucker watched me closely at the hotel and looked over the register carefully but there are a number of strangers at the hotel just now so he could not pick out one man more than another."[5]

Sayers met with Governor Thornton in his office the next morning and then headed to the penitentiary to interview Ely "Slick" Miller. The detective met Miller in Colonel Bergamer's office. Bergamer had already explained to Miller what Sayers wanted and he found Miller ready and willing to talk. Miller said he had been thinking over the matter since he made his first statement, which has been lost to history, but did not think he could give any additional information, except for one point he had overlooked. Miller said that at the time the Stock Growers' Association was formed and prior to the proposition of the 1894 murder plot, he was riding with Ed Brown from San Marcial to Brown's ranch when the conversation turned on the action of the Stock Growers' Association. Brown told Miller "he could get a man named Maxammeano Greago [Maximiano Griego] to kill W. C. McDonald for $100 and that he had a notion to do so."[6] William C. McDonald was the president of the Southeastern New Mexico Stock Growers' Association.[7] The interview continued. Miller did not know if Brown made the proposition to Griego, but said "that Greago [sic] was a tool in the hands of Ed. [sic] Brown and that Brown frequently used him to do his dirty work . . . ." When they decided to kill Fountain, Brown said he would hire a man to do his part, and Miller believed that man was Griego. Miller said Brown was "a shrewd cold blooded man and that he always looked for material among the Mexicans to do his dirty work; he was willing to pay for it and thought nothing of hiring a man to kill some one, but if it were possible he would avoid getting into it himself." Miller said "Greago was more closely connected with Brown than any one else, and that he was in a position to tell a good deal about him . . . ." Miller thought that because of Griego's current predicament (he had been convicted of murder) that Sayers might be able to get him to talk.

Miller told of other men connected with Brown in his cattle stealing: Tom Davenport, Charlie Allen, and Green Scott. But Miller did not think any of these men would say anything about Brown, particularly Scott, "who was about the only American that Brown was very confidential with."

Miller moved on to Oliver Lee and Bill McNew. He told Sayers, "Wm. McNew was completely under the control of Oliver Lee and anything that Lee told him to do he would do, believing that Lee could get him out of any trouble, but if McNew could be gotten away from Oliver Lee he would be easily broken down, as he was a very weak man in many ways, but in Miller's opinion nothing could be done with him so long as Lee was with him . . . ." Miller said that McNew "always wore boots and to the best of his recollection he used to run one of them over very badly at the heel." Miller went on to say that McNew was with Oliver Lee when Lee killed "the Frenchman" in Dog Canyon. Miller then told what he knew about that killing.

Miller stated that the Frenchman had some cattle at a ranch at Dog Canyon, close to Lee's ranch, and said he "was a cranky old man . . . ." When Lee rounded up cattle the Frenchman looked through them to see if there were any stolen cattle in the bunch. He threatened to have Lee indicted for stealing stock and Lee was afraid that he would and could furnish the proof. Miller heard Lee and McNew talking about it several times and heard Lee say he would kill him. The Frenchman eventually sold his cattle but stayed on his ranch and did a little farming. Whenever any of Lee's cattle approached his property, the Frenchman ran them off with his dogs. Lee again threatened to kill him. Finally, one day Lee, McNew, and a man named Dan Davis rode to the Frenchman's place. The Frenchman, with his gun, met them at the door. He "began cursing Lee," and Lee shot and killed him. "There was nothing done about it, as the Frenchman had no relatives and no friends to take the matter up, so Oliver Lee jumped his ranch and the matter ended." Miller's source of this story was Dan Davis.[8] "The Frenchman" Miller referred to was Francois (Frank) Jean Rochas, also known as "Frenchy," who was killed the day after Christmas 1894. No one went after his murderers.[9]

Miller pinned two other murders on Lee. He told the operative that Walter Good was killed by Lee and Tom Tucker. A man named "Cherokee" Bill Kellam was with them. Lee was afraid that Kellam would talk so he took him on a trip to Mexico to get some cattle. When Lee got him to a convenient place across the border, he killed Kellam. Miller had heard Lee "boasting about it afterwards, but does not know any way to prove it, as he only has Lee's own statement, but he is quite satisfied that these things are true."[10] To be fair to Lee, no other evidence seems to exist that Lee murdered Kellam.

However, Lee, Tucker, Jim Cooper, and Kellam were charged with Walter Good's murder. It never came to trial.[11]

Of James Gililland, Miller gave the opinion that he wouldn't talk, as "he is a young fellow that wants to be bad and he has a good deal of nerve." Miller thought the Fountain bodies were disposed of in the San Andreas Mountains, "as he says that country is full of caves and deep ravines where no one ever goes and the work could be done in such a way as to leave no trail."

When Sayers returned to town, Thornton arranged for him to receive a commission as deputy U. S. marshall for Doña Ana County. While taking the oath, he noticed that Tom Tucker was watching him and seemed very interested. Sayers reported, "He made it convenient to follow me and wait around to see what I was there for."

Sayers left that night for Socorro.[12]

Socorro, winter 1885. The courthouse is the tall building left of center. (Courtesy of New Mexico State University Library, Archives and Special Collections, No. 03630474.)

ten

Ed Brown

After arriving in Socorro, William Sayers learned that Maximiano Griego, the man Miller claimed Brown would hire to kill McDonald, was in jail at the time of the Fountain murder. This information originated from a man named Doherty, who also stated that Brown allegedly had said that he could find the bodies. Sayers reported, "Mr. Doherty is quite positive that Brown did not kill Fountain, but he is equally certain that Brown knows all about the affair."

From Doherty and Elfego Baca, Sayers learned that Green Scott had left the C. N. ranch to, as he claimed, attend court in Lincoln, and returned after the murder of Fountain. Doherty and Baca were both in Lincoln at that time and did not see Scott there. Baca said he spoke to Scott once about the killing and "Scott said he was glad of it and wished to God they had gotten the rest of the family." Sayers learned that a man named Punch Williams was the main witness against Scott in a cattle rustling charge, but Williams had since disappeared and was said to have been killed by Scott. With Williams gone, the charges had been dropped.[1]

The next day Sayers met with Socorro County Sheriff Holm O. Bursum and said of him, "I found Mr. Bursum a very intelligent man and he seems to know the people here thoroughly."[2] Bursum told Sayers that he had heard the story told by José Angel Gallegos (regarding Brown, Scott, and a third man returning to Brown's ranch and noted by Fraser in his reports of March 16 and 17) and knew where he had heard it, but Bursum "did not think it was quite straight because he could not get any one to corroborate the statement that Green Scott was with Brown when Brown left his ranch and Scott certainly did not return to the ranch with Brown. . . ." Bursum said that Ed Brown came into San Marcial a few days after Colonel Fountain was killed and his horse was in bad shape. He added that there was a man with him whose name he had not yet learned, but whose horse was completely "done out and was said to have lain down as soon as he was put in a stable . . . ." Bursum's information came from Deputy Donaldson Walker, who was at one time a cattle thief and a good friend of Brown's. Bursum had "been able to render him a number of favors in times past and got him out of some serious troubles so that Walker is devoted to him and will do anything for him." A short time after the Fountains disappeared, Ed Brown had told Walker that he could fix it so that Walker could earn the reward that was offered for the recovery of the bodies.

Bursum told Sayers that a man named McKee believed he saw Ed Brown's horse in Rincon the day before Brown got to San Marcial. He was thought to have come up by way of Rincon. Bursum believed he had men who could "get a squeal out of Brown."[3]

Sayers left Socorro with Sheriff Bursum the next morning and traveled to San Marcial, where they called on Don Walker. Walker related the conversation he had with Ed Brown about the note. According to Walker, Brown said, "You remember the man that wanted you to get bonds on that cattle stealing case?"

Walker replied, "Yes."

"Well," Brown said, "I can give you a letter to him and he will fix it so you can find Fountain's body all right, he knows all about it."

"Walker said all right and it was settled that whenever Walker was ready to go Brown would give him this letter." Walker said he knew the man Brown referred to but could not recall his name. Walker said the man had only one eye. Sayers "asked him if he would remember the name if he heard it and he said yes," so Sayers "asked him if the man had not gone under the soubriquet of 'Goodeye' and he said yes . . . ." Sayers then "mentioned a number of names of men in that country," and when he got to the name William Carr, Walker stopped him and said that was the man. "Carr was the name he could not remember and now he knew all about the bonds. Carr wanted him to help and get bonds for a man who was in jail, a friend of Carr's, and Walker had refused as he was not in a position to do so."

Walker said Brown told him that the men who were ahead of Fountain on the road were not the men who killed him, that they only led Fountain into the trap. Brown said, "the boy was all right and was not killed. Walker said that Brown made these statements like a man who had some knowledge of what he was talking about, but at the same time Brown might have been simply giving it as his opinion for he often spoke in that positive way about things of which he had no personal knowledge."

Sayers next met with Dr. Cruickshank, who told him that the previous Thursday, April 16, he had had a long talk with Ed Brown. Brown brought up the Fountain matter, "saying that he had been informed by Mr. Perry that there were some stories afloat about horses having left his ranch before the murder and that they had been traced back to his place and that he was suspected of being mixed up in it . . . ." Brown said "he cared nothing about the suspicion," but believed if any one could find the bodies he could. "He said it was an outrage to kill the child and he thought it would be an easy matter to work the matter up and get the men after the bodies were found." Sayers noted that Cruickshank told him "he believed that Brown was sincere and he could do more toward finding the bodies than anyone else."[4]

That same day, April 20, Sayers took the sworn deposition of William Steen, who had witnessed some suspicious activity by Ed Brown and Emerald James. Steen stated that on Monday, February 3, 1896, he was attending to the corral and stable of S. J. Hanna in San Marcial. At about 5 o'clock that evening Ed Brown and Emerald James rode into the corral and unsaddled their horses. Steen said that the horses were completely tired out and both animals lay down as soon as the saddles were removed. Steen remarked to Brown that they must have been riding very hard and asked where he had come from. "Brown answered both questions, saying they had come from across the river and acknowledged he had been riding hard."

Steen then asked Ed Brown if he had heard of Colonel Fountain's murder or disappearance. Brown stated that he had not, and asked what Steen knew about it, whereupon Steen told him that it was in the newspaper. Brown asked where the paper was and subsequently got a paper in Mr. S. J. Hanna's store. After reading the account in the paper, Brown remarked "that there was nothing in that and that they had not gotten descriptions of the murderers." Steen had noticed when Ed Brown dismounted that he was wearing boots and that both of the heels had been cut or chopped off. He "noticed that this had been done quite recently as the nails which fastened the boot heel on were sticking out and the leather was quite fresh looking; showing that the boot had not come in contact with the ground very much since the heel had been taken off." Steen mentioned to Brown that his boot heels were chopped off and added, "a plan like that would have been a good one for the men who killed Fountain to adopt, as the paper stated that the tracks around Col. Fountain's buggy all showed high heels." Ed Brown did not say anything in response and, according to Steen, "seem to be somewhat worried at his remark . . . ." Emerald James did not take any part in the conversation and left without saying a word to Steen.

Steen described the horses ridden by Brown and James as follows: "One was [a] small sorrel horse," and the other was a large brown horse. He said "that both animals were too tired to eat and refused food for some time after they came to the corral."

Steen did not notice any arms on Brown or James.[5]

Sayers was able to confirm that Brown and James were in San Marcial on February 3 and 4, for they signed the registry at the boarding house. Sayers wrote, "I finished up my reports to date and send [sent] them in by Express as I did not like to trust the office here; the people in it seem altogether too curious."[6]

After spending the last few days looking, Sayers finally tracked down Ed Brown and Emerald James. He saw the two at 5 p.m. and after they had corralled their cattle, Sayers got Dr. Cruickshank to come down and introduce them. They stood on the street and talked for a few minutes. Sayers reported, "Brown said he believed he could be of some help in this matter but said he did not want to be seen in conference with me on the street and that he would not have these men in town get on to him for anything, but he would meet me after supper and talk the matter over . . . ."

Brown, the thirty-eight- or thirty-nine-year-old former Texan, met Sayers in his room for about three hours that evening.[7] Brown told Sayers

> that he had been joshing with Dr. Crookshanks [Cruickshank] about looking up this murder, and that in one way he was in earnest; he believed if any man could find the body he could, and he gave it as his opinion that once the body was found it would be an easy matter for him to get the rest and he would get the information and turn it over to the officers so that they could do the rest and get all concerned provided he could get half the reward. In order to do this and assist him he suggested to Dr. Crookshanks that some one post a reward in the papers for say $5,000 for the recovery of the body, and let it be put in at once and the people in Dona [Doña] Ana County would read it and talk a good

deal about it and then he would go over there and get among those fellows and use this argument, that some of them might just as well have that reward as not, and as he had their confidence he believed that he could get one of them to tell him where it was, on condition that he (Brown) would split the reward with the party giving the information, and then he said "as soon as they show me the body it will come quite natural to talk over how it was carried there and how the killing was done so that I can get all the information at one time if I get any at all."

Brown said "he used to live in Dona [Doña] Ana County and was intimately acquainted with all the men in the Organ and Sacramento Mts. and that none of them would suspect him for a moment; and he knows that if either of three parties he has in mind did the work or knows of it that he can get all the details and do it easily." For some time he did not say who these men were, "but in the end he said that he figured on Bill McNew, Wm. Carr, and Jack Tucker." Brown "went on to say that if Oliver Lee, McNew, Tom Tucker, and Carr killed that boy they were no longer his friends. He said he had two boys of his own and he did not want to think that either of them might be killed for some crime he might do or because some one had it in for him that the child should be killed for convenience sake and any man who could kill a child was too dangerous to be let remain at liberty."

Sayers mentioned to Brown that there had been some stories connecting him with Fountain's disappearance. Brown "said he knew about it, but did not care as they were all false . . . ." Sayers took a statement of Brown's whereabouts at the time of the disappearance. Brown took a starting point from a date he could remember. He said that on the twentieth of January he went to Engle for a load of corn. He took his wife with him. In Engle, Colonel Mothersill asked him when he was going to round up some cattle he had bought from Mothersill, and Brown said he would come as soon as he got home with his corn. On the way home he met John Carter who told him that Tom O'Donnell had some steers for him at Mound Spring. He returned to his ranch on the twenty-fourth. On about January 25 or 26, he went with a man named Thergood, who worked for him, down to Mothersill's ranch and gathered the cattle there. He said he worked several days and did not remember how long, but thought he got back to his ranch about the twenty-ninth. "He brought the cattle to Thergood's corral and put them in there and afterwards turned them loose as he concluded it would not pay him to take them at the figure Col. Mothersill asked . . . ." Brown then went with Emerald James to Mound Spring to get the cattle from O'Donnell. They drove the cattle to the Mocking Bird Spring, camped there all night, and returned next day. He thought he might have been at Mound Spring on the first of February, but was unsure of the exact date. He did not remember what he did on his return to the ranch but was sure he did not go any place for several days.

Sayers asked Brown where he was when he first heard of Fountain's murder. Brown said he was at Thergood's place, where he heard it from Harry Crawford when he brought the mail. Sayers asked him how long this was after the murder and Brown said about a week, because Crawford had the eastern papers and the murder was written up in them. Brown went on to say that the date of his going to Mothersill's ranch could easily be established as he arrived there the same day as one of the directors of the company from Colorado and a black employee was discharged. As to the time he was at Mound Spring, he said that Tom O'Donnell or Randolph Reynolds, who was there at the time, might know when that was. "[A]t any rate Brown says that he believes he can show where he was every day during that time and he cares nothing about the stories that may have been circulated . . . ." Sayers reported that he "questioned him very closely about coming in here at any time with played out horses and he positively" stated that he did not come any time "with tired stock," and anyone who said he did was lying.

Sayers observed

> I noticed in talking with Brown that he always used the word body and not bodies when speaking [of] Col. Fountain and his son, and at first he was very nervous but soon got his self possession, he has studied the situation closely and is a very shrewd man in his way, but the whole drift of his conversation seemed to be to make some sort of an arrangement by which he could be made safe himself and then he would be willing to do something for the side of the law. He said if he did not succeed in doing anything in the matter he would be willing to tell all he could and give all the pointers he could think of but he wanted to try for himself first.[8]

The next day Sayers received a statement from Emerald James that was similar to Brown's, although James could not remember any dates. He said he was with Brown every day in late January and early February and denied that they ever came into San Marcial with tired horses. James said he hunted down a man named Ely, who had a shop in town, and the dates in Ely's books showed that James and Brown dropped off cattle on February 1.

While Sayers was speaking with James, Brown came down the street and called to him. When he came over, Sayers told him, "I have been talking with Mr. James about where he was on the 1st of February and [he] tells me about the trip you made to Mound Spring and that it was possible you were over there then."

James said, "Yes, I thought so but I was mistaken because Ely has a date on his book that shows that we were here on the first with cattle."

Brown looked very surprised and said it could not be possible, that Ely must be wrong and that they could not have been there then. He said to James, "Don't you remember when I came from Engle with the corn that I met John Carter and he told me Tom O'Donnell had some cattle for me and I sent for you that night and the next day we went to Mound Spring, got two head of steers from Tom O'Donnell and came back to the ranch and brought the steers into town, that was before we went to Mothersill's and when we went back we went to Good Fortune and gathered the steers there."

While Brown talked, James watched him closely and agreed to everything he said. James then stated that it was hard to remember dates when a man was on a ranch. Both men began arguing about the trip to Mothersill's until James finally said, "Well you know we wrote some letters there at Engle and we know who we wrote to and could get those letters back so that the dates will show."

Brown and James disagreed as to when they first heard of the killing as well. Brown said that Crawford brought the news, but James claimed it was Thergood. They did both agree that they heard about it at Thergood's and it was ten or twelve days after the murder of Colonel Fountain.

Sayers later spoke with a man named Harry Crawford, who said that when he read the news at the ranch from the *St. Louis Republic*, everyone seemed surprised by Fountain's murder.

After that, Don Walker approached Sayers with more information about Ely. Walker told Sayers that Ely had said to him, "I don't want to go to Sayers, but you can tell him that if the indictments against Brown in the cattle stealing cases are quashed by the Governor, that Brown will dig up some information on the Fountain matter." Walker had asked Ely why he would not tell

Sayers himself, and Ely responded that he would not do so and did not intend to mix up in the affair at all, but he knew this much and wanted Sayers to know it.

Sayers later learned that Brown went to Burham's store and bought a new pair of boots when he came in and had demanded a discount because the soles had come off his last pair. Brown traded there regularly and received the discount. There was no date next to the transaction in the books.[9]

Sayers wired the governor, then left that night to meet him in Socorro the next morning and discuss Brown. They thought Brown could be made to talk, and finally decided that Brown would be arrested on the cattle stealing charge of which he was to be tried the next month. They didn't believe Brown could supply the bond and could be kept until court opened. Thornton thought it should be worked out quietly and that Pat Garrett or anyone else in Doña Ana County should not be informed of this plan.[10]

Sayers headed back down to San Marcial the next day. Before he had left San Marcial, Sayers had checked the brand books and receipts in Ely's shop when Ely had stepped out. Sayers found no entry on February 1 for any cattle received by Brown, only an entry for the twelfth, but Sayers did not check all of his books at this time. On his return to San Marcial, he went back to Ely's shop and asked to see his books. Ely showed them to Sayers and on the ledger Sayers found an entry of two head of cattle brought from Ed Brown on the first day of February. "[T]he entry was made in pencil and looked quite fresh; the entry before that was on the 11th of Feb. and after the 28th . . . ." Sayers asked Ely for his blotter which he thought should correspond with the ledger, but it did not. The same two head of cattle were marked in the blotter as brought in on February 13. Ely thought the blotter was correct. He said he must have neglected to put down the three after the one, and stated that the bill of sale would correspond with the blotter. Sayers asked him for the brand book and receipts. The bill of sale and the brand book showed the same cattle marked down for February 13. Sayers said that "Ely was confused by the way I questioned him and I finally told him he would have to keep his hands off this business altogether and that he did not stand in a very good light himself. I also told him not to touch that entry, but let it stand as it is."

Sayers followed with a visit to S. Hanna and examined his books, but found no entry in them for February 3, 4, or 5. Hanna told Sayers "that Brown and James came in about that time with played out horses and put up in his corral . . . ."[11]

On Sunday, April 26, Sayers spoke to Colonel Mothersill. He noted that the colonel was accurate with dates because he kept a diary. Mothersill confirmed that on or about January 20 Ed Brown came to Engle and bought a load of corn from him. They had some talk about Brown gathering some cattle for Mothersill. On January 25, Brown came to Mothersill's Good Fortune ranch with Thergood and Emerald James. When Colonel Mothersill left the ranch on the twenty-seventh, Brown, James, and Thergood were still there. Brady, the man who was in charge of the ranch at the time, said that Brown, James, and Thergood stayed there for two or three more days. They left Wednesday evening or Thursday morning, which would be January 29 or 30. Brown did not take any steers with him when he left Good Fortune.

Mothersill said that he and a man named Holmes returned to Good Fortune and then visited some other ranches. They ate dinner on the first of February at Summerford's place at Leasburg. One of the men who worked for Mothersill, Hiram Yost, was there. "Yost told the Col. on this occasion that he looked to see some trouble on the other side before long. (He meant the east side of the San Andreas Mts.)" Mothersill added that he also saw Frank Hill that day.

Sayers also noted that Mothersill had just received a letter from Ed Brown asking if he remembered the date that Brown was at Engle.[12]

The next few days were uneventful for operative Sayers. Then Ed Brown was arrested. Sayers commented, "Ed Brown takes the matter cool, but he is under the impression that he can get a new bond."[13] Brown was being held in the jail on the second floor of the Socorro Courthouse building. Sayers paid Brown a visit and they talked for two hours. Brown was hoping to get out in time to keep an appointment to receive cattle on the sixth, and was sure his bond would be accepted. Sayers reported of the meeting:

> I talked with him about this bond for some time, and then when he led off on the Fountain murder I explained to him that I had called on Gov. Thornton as Brown had requested and placed his proposition before the Governor, but I found that the matter was in an altogether different light. I then went ahead and outlined the evidence which I claimed the Gov. had collected and intimated that the information came from Chas. Spence, but did not mention any names. Brown let me go all through, and then just laughed at the whole thing and said that any one who ever said that he did at any time speak of killing Col. Fountain or any other member of the Stock Association, was lying and could not prove a word of it.

Brown told Sayers that after he was indicted he not only wrote several letters to Fountain, but also "had a friend of his who was a warm personal friend of Col. Fountain's go to the Col. and talk to him about the cases against him and that Col. Fountain sent him word by this mutual friend that he need not worry any, but to go ahead and attend to his business, that the cases would not be pushed." "Now," Brown said, "is it likely that after a man had sent me such a message as that that I would make an attempt to kill him." Brown did not give the man's name, "but said he could get him on the stand to swear to this at any time and that this man was at the present time doing all he could to assist in uncovering Fountain's murderers." Brown's claim of the correspondence with Fountain does seem very possible. Brown obviously wasn't that hard to find, yet he wasn't arrested and brought into court when Ely Miller and the rest of his gang were tried.

Sayers's report continued:

> He repeated his statement that these men, Carr, McNew, Tucker, Lee and others in Dona [Doña] Ana County were all good friends of his, but if they had done this job he wanted to know it and would very willingly turn the thing up, as such men were too dangerous to live with. Brown makes a strong talk on this head and he then said it makes no difference to him whether he can or cannot prove his whereabouts at the time of the murder, he knows he was not there and that he cannot be convicted for a crime that he did not commit. So far as his being able to make a statement now, he claims he cannot do so and that all he could say would be to give his opinion which would be of no more value than that of any man who had read the newspaper accounts, and he positively would not tell any lies for the purpose of getting out of his present difficulties as they would be proven to be lies and then he would have no friends left at all . . . .[14]

Sayers got nowhere with Brown the rest of the day and evening. The next day plans were made for Thornton to come down with "Slick" Miller. Sayers visited Brown in the morning and made a statement about him being connected to the murder, again without mentioning his sources. Brown responded, "Of course some one may have gone to Governor Thornton and made a statement implicating me, but it is a lie, the chances are good that it is some one who is in a hard hole, probably in the Pen., and who would make any sort of a statement in order to get executive clemency . . . ."[15] Brown knew precisely the situation his accuser was in.

The next few days brought no change in Brown. Even when Miller gave his statement in front of him, Brown did not change his story.[16] After talking over the matter with Doherty, Thornton began to change his opinion on Brown, and now believed he was not present at the murder of Fountain and his son and even believed "it is possible he may not have been in the last deal at all . . . ." As it looked like Brown would be let out of jail anyway, he decided it was best to let him go and see what he could find out.[17]

Brown was released. Nothing else new developed from the Sayers end of the case. On May 12, Thornton told Sayers that he had written to McParland to recall him. Sayers was told he'd be brought back in when Ed Brown returned to Socorro for trial, but he was not.[18] He arrived in Denver May 14 and the Pinkerton end of the investigation officially ended.[19]

Two days later, the entire file of the Pinkerton reports was stolen from the governor's office.[20]

eleven

Indictments

Garrett and Perry began the next month working on Luis Herrera (a different Herrera than was with the search party) after they received information that he might know where the bodies were, but this led to nothing.[1]

Not much progress was made in the investigation or the search for the bodies over the next two years. Fall, meanwhile, was able to have the cattle rustling indictments Fountain had brought against Lee and McNew dropped.[2]

Pat Garrett had to run in the fall elections of 1896 in order to keep the office of sheriff. Garrett was a loyal, lifelong Democrat, but owed his position to the Republicans. Torn, Garrett decided to run as an Independent and then registered as a Republican after an easy win.[3]

In the meantime, life went on in New Mexico. William Llewellyn served as a delegate in the Territorial Republican Convention and was elected to the Territorial House of Representatives, of which he became speaker.[4] James Gililland married.[5] So did Thomas Branigan.[6] Oliver Lee was a delegate for the Territorial Democratic Convention in 1896, and in early 1898, he sold one of his ranches to Charles Eddy for the purpose of running a new railroad through. The land Lee sold Eddy became the city of Alamogordo.[7] Albert Fall served on the Territorial Council and served as Territorial Solicitor General, only to be removed (with some difficulty, as Fall refused to resign) by the new man in Santa Fe, Miguel Otero.[8]

William Thornton resigned as the governor of the New Mexico Territory in April 1897. Newly elected President William McKinley appointed prominent New Mexican Miguel A. Otero as the territory's new Governor, a post that he served until 1906.[9]

During this time, little was done to bring Fountain's killers to justice. Fountain's friends and family pressured Garrett to act, for as time passed, key witnesses were dying, disappearing, or suffering memory loss. Les Dow, for one, was murdered in Eddy. Dave Kemp was tried and acquitted for Dow's murder.[10]

Garrett had a clear opinion of who the guilty parties were. He attributed the lack of action to his concern that Fall would be able to shield his friends from indictments.[11] As a result, nothing of consequence took place in the investigation, from the summer of 1896 until the spring of 1898.

Governor Otero urged action in the Fountain case. As April 1 approached, the date that the grand jury was to meet, rumors swirled that indictments would be sought.[12] With all of the gossip swirling, an interesting incident happened in Tobe Tipton's saloon in Tularosa. Tobe Tipton, Albert Fall, Oliver Lee, George Curry, and Jeff Sanders were in the back room playing poker when Pat Garrett walked in. Garrett was in town to notify jurors of the upcoming term of court. Tipton invited Garrett to join the game. The sheriff accepted and took the open seat, right across from Lee. The game lasted for three straight days and nights. A player might drop out for a meal or a nap, but the game never stopped. With players getting up and down, they changed seats frequently, all except Oliver Lee and Pat Garrett, who sat directly opposite each other and never changed places. The men spoke sparingly.[13] Tipton said years later that "there was more dynamite gathered around that poker table than could be found in any other room in New Mexico."[14]

It was George Curry who broke the silence. "I've been hearing that the Doña Ana County grand jury is going to indict somebody in this crowd for doing away with the Fountains. My guess is that somebody in this bunch may want to hire a lawyer before long, and I have an idea that the lawyer he is going to hire might be sitting in this here game." Nobody said a word.

Then Lee looked at Garrett. "Mr. Sheriff, if you wish to serve any papers on me at any time, I will be here or out to the ranch."

"All right, Mr. Lee," Garrett responded. "If any papers are to be served on you, I will mail them to you or send them to George Curry here to serve on you." With that, Garrett left and headed to his Las Cruces home.[15]

Lee went to Las Cruces too, staying at Henry Stoes's store, so he could be on hand if the grand jury indicted him. The grand jury met and adjourned without even mentioning Lee's name.[16] As soon as Lee left Las Cruces, however, Garrett appeared before Judge Frank Parker to request bench warrants for Oliver Lee, Bill McNew, James Gililland, and Bill Carr. In Garrett's deposition, he promised to show that "Oliver M. Lee, William McNew, and James Gililland are the parties who murdered Colonel Albert J. Fountain and his son, Henry Fountain." He also presented a second affidavit signed by Thomas Branigan and William Llewellyn, stating that they found tracks pointing to Lee, McNew, Carr, and Gililland. Parker issued the warrants.[17]

The following day Garrett arrested McNew and Carr without trouble. Lee and Gililland were a different story. Lee had ridden back in to Las Cruces, to Henry Stoes's store, to pick up clothes he had left there. He told Stoes before he rode out of town that he didn't intend to be arrested. "Pat Garrett will shoot me in the back if he ever arrests me, and will claim it was self-defense."[18]

Lee went to his Dog Canyon ranch, and then on to El Paso, where he told the *El Paso Times* that he "did not propose to be taken to Las Cruces and kept in jail for an indefinite length of time."[19] This seemed to be a more likely reason for avoiding arrest than his claim that he was afraid Garrett would kill him.

In the meantime, Carr and McNew were held without bail.[20] As Garrett waited for the right moment to go after Lee, people began to talk. They said the man who could only kill Billy the Kid in a darkened bedroom was now afraid to go after Lee. The truth is, Garrett was in no hurry to arrest Lee. He hoped he could keep McNew and Carr in jail and get one or both to talk.

Fall worked quickly to get the pair out of jail. He enlisted the services of two powerful attorneys, Judge H. L. Warren from Albuquerque, who was an experienced trial lawyer, and Harry Daugherty, the district attorney from Socorro County, an office from which he resigned to have time to work on the case. The preliminary hearing began just seven days after McNew and Carr were incarcerated. Doña Ana County's prosecuting attorney Richmond P. Barnes saw how big this was and called in two Republican heavyweights, William B. Childers and Thomas B. Catron, to assist the prosecution.[21] Just before the preliminary hearing began, Tom Tucker, in town to attend the trial of his friends, was arrested for a separate murder.[22]

The hearing got under way on the ninth day of April 1898. The courtroom was packed with armed men. Thirty-eight-year-old Judge Frank W. Parker ordered all persons carrying weapons, with the exception of the sheriff and his deputies, to leave. No one moved.[23]

The first witness the prosecution called was Jack Maxwell. Maxwell, who was expected to be a key witness, disappointed. He testified that he was at Lee's Dog Canyon ranch about the time of the Fountains' murders and that Lee, McNew, and Gililland rode in together while he was there, but he was no longer able to remember days or dates. He would later admit that he was drunk when he testified.

On cross-examination Fall tore into the inebriated Maxwell. Maxwell admitted that he had told different stories to different people. In the end, according to the *El Paso Times*, Maxwell "succeeded in contradicting his direct testimony and proving himself a good witness for the defense."[24]

The first day's testimony, which was purely circumstantial, was meant to show that Carr shadowed Fountain from Lincoln to La Luz and then notified waiting men, who rode down and intercepted the Fountains as they passed Chalk Hill.

Following this first day, the *Silver City Independent* reported, "an attempt was made to tamper with one of the witnesses for the prosecution, but Sheriff Garrett appeared upon the scene at the proper time and blocked the game, and the party who was endeavoring to lead the witness astray is said to have been rather roughly handled."[25]

Captain Thomas Branigan was called to the stand on the second day. Branigan stated that he was one of the posse that went out after receiving the news of Fountain's disappearance. Branigan testified to the finding of Colonel Fountain's abandoned buckboard. He said he found a number of footprints around the buckboard, some of which were made by high-heeled cowboy boots, and others that were made by the shoes of a small child. It was reported that Branigan "created somewhat of a sensation" when he stated that sometime later, when he saw Bill McNew in Las Cruces, he measured McNew's footprints very carefully and they corresponded in every way with measurements he had taken of a set of footprints around the buckboard. On cross-examination by Fall, it was reported that Branigan "was somewhat confused" but that his testimony "was not materially affected."[26]

Carl Clausen led off the next day's testimony. He told of following the trail to Lee's Wildy Well ranch and of his run-in with Lee while there. Clausen identified McNew as one of the men inside the ranch house. William Llewellyn then described leading the search party. His testimony corroborated the previous testimony of Branigan. Llewellyn also stated that he was with Captain Branigan when Branigan measured McNew's footprints in Las Cruces.[27]

Eugene Van Patten testified that he had led a posse from Las Cruces. He testified that he found a pool of blood by the side of the main road just south of Chalk Hill and an impression as though a body had been thrown from a buggy. He said he gathered a quantity of the blood-soaked sand. At this point, two blood-stained coins and a napkin were exhibited.

Kent Kearney told of a conversation he had had with James Gililland, in which Gililland said of Fountain, "Don't you think the country is better and quieter since the son of a bitch was killed?" Gililland also told Kearney "that he thought it was a very slick job and that he had watched the searching parties at work."[28]

The next day brought B. F. Wooton and Charles Meyer to the stand, both to testify that they had seen Carr in La Luz on February 1, 1896. Meyer said that Carr came to his La Luz store every few days. Next came Pat Garrett, who was on the stand for a total of five minutes and said nothing of value. Court adjourned early that day as the prosecution was waiting for witnesses to arrive.[29] The trial resumed two days later.[30]

Dr. Joseph Blazer took the stand early the next day of the trial. Blazer spoke of Fountain's stay at his home on January 30, 1896. Blazer had seen two men pass his home, but did not see their faces. James Gould was next. Gould said that he was working at Bill McNew's ranch on February 1, 1896. McNew was not there on the first. Gould said that about a week earlier James Gililland had come to the ranch for cartridges and told Gould that if anyone asked for him to say he had gone to Roswell. Gililland instead rode in the direction of Dog Canyon. Gould did not see Gililland again until four or five days after Fountain's disappearance. Gould said that sometime later Gililland told him how Lee, McNew, and himself had watched the searching parties, and Gililland said of Fountain, "the old son of a bitch had left Texas in a chicken coop and raised hell everywhere he went but wouldn't raise anymore."[31]

The next witness, Riley Baker, spoke of a conversation that he had had with Gililland about a year after the disappearance. Gililland pointed out the place where he had watched the parties search for Fountain. Baker said that when he commented that the killing of a child was a horrible murder, Gililland responded that Henry Fountain "was a half-breed, and he did not know whether he was any better than a dog." Gililland went on to say that "if a body had to be found before anybody could be convicted, it would be a long time before anyone could be."[32]

The first witness, Jack Maxwell, was recalled. He repeated his earlier testimony, but was not as rattled by Fall this time around. Still, Fall managed to make Maxwell a good witness for the defense. He got Maxwell to testify that he had been promised a share of the $10,000 reward, $2,000, if his testimony led to a conviction of Fountain's murderers. Although it is not uncommon to offer a reward in exchange for evidence, Fall made it sound suspiciously like a bribe.[33] When the prosecution then closed its case, the defense introduced no new evidence.

With all of the evidence in, Parker released Carr, stating that there was insufficient evidence against him. McNew was held in jail, without bond, and ordered to appear before the next grand jury.[34] Garrett hoped he would confess while in jail, but the confession never came.[35]

William McNew
(Date and photographer unknown.
Reprint from Sonnichsen, *Tularosa: Last of the Frontier West*. Image used courtesy of University of New Mexico Press.)

twelve

Shootout at Wildy Well

Shortly after the hearing, Fall temporarily left New Mexico. As a captain in Company D, New Mexico Volunteers, Fall joined the Spanish-American War. Although he did not go to Cuba and fight in the war, he stayed out of New Mexico for the time being.[1] An interesting side note was the endorsements Fall received in his quest to be a captain in the war. One letter of endorsement that came to Governor Otero was signed by Numa Reymond, Fred Bascom, John McFie, John Riley, and Pat Garrett.[2] Judging from all surviving documents, no one else received the number of endorsements that Fall did, and none of his were from expected Fall supporters. It was obvious that what they really wanted was to get Fall out of New Mexico.

Also leaving for the war was William Llewellyn, who was captain of Troop G in the regiment that would become known as Roosevelt's Rough Riders. Llewellyn became a lifelong friend of Theodore Roosevelt. During the Rough Riders' charge up San Juan Hill, Llewellyn contracted yellow fever and was sent to a hospital in New York.[3]

Things began to look up for Garrett. With McNew behind bars, he was able to be patient in his pursuit of Lee and Gililland. He went on searches for them a few times, at least once at the end of April and once in June[4], but didn't track them down until July 10, 1898. Lee and Gililland had been hiding out in the desert, with beards fully grown for disguise. Two of Garrett's deputies ran into them at W. W. Cox's ranch. They did not try to arrest them, and the fugitives did not seem troubled by their presence. As deputies Clint Llewellyn and José Espalin left, Espalin purportedly warned Lee to be careful. Espalin then rode to Garrett's ranch to tell Garrett where the fugitives were.[5]

Garrett quickly put together a posse consisting of Ben Williams, Kent Kearney, Clint Llewellyn, and Espalin. Kearney was not a regular deputy but felt a sense of duty to do all he could. They set out in the evening and found the tracks of the wanted men that led to Lee's Wildy Well ranch. The posse stopped about a mile from Wildy Well and continued on foot.

The land was flat with the nearest mountain range visible to the east. Wildy Well consisted of an adobe house with an attached wagon shed, corral, pump house, outbuildings, windmill, and a large water tank on a platform with dirt piled up high around the bottom. It was about four in the morning and still dark when they arrived. Without anything nearby, it was certainly dead quiet in the empty desert. As the group approached, Espalin removed his boots to walk more quietly. When they reached the doorstep, they could hear snoring inside the house. With Kearney following, Garrett opened the unlocked door and rushed in, swiftly thrusting the barrel of his six-shooter into the ribs of the nearest sleeping figure while ordering them to throw up their hands. The person was Mary Madison, who jumped up and screamed. Her husband James Madison, the three Madison children, and a guest named Dennis McVeigh all awoke. Garrett asked where Lee and Gililland were. He received no answer. Garrett and his men then searched the outbuildings. As they searched, McVeigh was seen attempting to signal someone on the adobe's flat roof, where it turned out Lee and Gililland had slept. Garrett ordered McVeigh to climb up and tell the pair to surrender. McVeigh refused. Garrett entered the house and ordered James Madison to go up and tell them to surrender. Madison refused.

With no other choice, Garrett positioned his men for a possible fight. With the sun beginning to rise, Garrett placed his men to the east, forcing Lee and Gililland to face the sun if there was a gunfight. The roof, which protected Lee and Gililland with two-foot adobe walls, would be a hard place to penetrate. Llewellyn was sent to guard the people in the house. Williams took shelter behind the water tank. Garrett, followed by Kearney and Espalin, climbed a ladder to the top of the shed that was attached to the house. With Espalin behind, Garrett and Kearney approached the roof on which Lee and Gililland slept. Was it possible that all of the commotion below had not woken Lee or Gililland? The pair claimed that they were asleep when Garrett shouted the order to surrender. Whether the inexperienced Deputy Kearney saw Lee or Gililland go for their guns when they awoke, or he just panicked, Kearney opened fire after the call to surrender. He said that the moment he saw Lee and Gililland, they were aiming their rifles at him and he fired. Either way, Lee and Gililland quickly had the rifles they slept with ready for use. Garrett fired after Kearney. Two bullets hit the roof just under Lee's stomach. Garrett ducked as a shot from Lee's Winchester flew right by where his head had been, making Lee think he had hit the sheriff. Kearney was shot twice, once in his shoulder and once in his groin. He tumbled off the roof to the ground. Espalin left the roof, but not before a passing bullet burned the flesh of his thigh. He was pinned against the house, unable to help without stepping into the line of fire. Lee reportedly laughed as he fought. It was said that anyone who heard Oliver Lee laugh never forgot it. Williams shot towards the roof from the water tank. Lee and Gililland in turn filled the tank full of lead. The cold water poured out on Williams, then suddenly all was quiet.

Lee and Gililland were in a veritable fortress compared to Garrett's posse. Their bodies were never exposed. All the sheriff's posse had to shoot at were a few small holes from cracks in the adobe, which Lee and Gililland used to shoot through. If any of the posse put themselves in a position to shoot at the holes, Lee and Gililland would have clear targets.[6]

Lee broke the silence. "You are a hell of a lot of bastards to shoot at a man when he is asleep."

"Kearney fired too quick," Garrett acknowledged, the sound of his voice surprising Lee, who thought he had shot the sheriff. "Are any of you hurt?" Garrett asked.

Lee replied, "No."

Garrett asked them to surrender.

"I don't think I will," Lee told him. "I've heard that you intend to kill me."

Garrett assured Lee that they would be perfectly safe in his hands. He again called on them to surrender.

"Pat," Lee said, "don't you think you've got the worst of this?"

"Don't you think I know it?"[7]

Lee then offered a cease-fire. Garrett and his men would be allowed to pull off and get help for Kearney, who was still on the ground, wounded. Garrett wasn't sure whether to believe Lee or not. Lee told Garrett that whenever he gave his word he kept it. Pat had no choice but to accept the offer. As they walked off, Lee yelled to Garrett that he would come in and surrender if Garrett could fix bond for him.

Garrett replied that he had nothing to do with his bond.

Garrett, along with Llewellyn, Williams, and Espalin, walked away. Williams was soaked. Espalin swore as thorns and cactus stickers stuck in his bootless feet.[8] Lee said years later of hearing Espalin "have a hard time of it," that, in spite of everything that just happened, "I just had to laugh." Garrett undoubtedly had his head down as he walked away from his biggest failure as a sheriff.[9]

The posse rode a few miles to Turquoise Siding, where Garrett sent a note back to Wildy Well: "Lee, how is Kearney. There is no telegraph station here. If you think Kearney can get well I will send to La Luz to get him a doctor. Garrett."[10] Garrett sent a section crew back for Kearney. By the time they got there, Lee and Gililland had either left or were possibly still hiding on the roof. Mary Madison removed the bullet from Kearney's groin. The Madison family saved the bullet.

Garrett took Kearney to Alamogordo that afternoon. Kearney was described as being cheerful the very next day, and was quoted as saying that he was "going to get well and go back and get those fellows." However, Kent Kearney, an important witness who had testified in the McNew-Carr preliminary hearing to an incriminating conversation with Gililland, died the following day. Lee and Gililland were indicted for the murder.[11]

Gililland and Lee went back into hiding, but this didn't stop Lee from communicating with the territory's newspapers. Lee sent a letter of his version of the Wildy Well fight to Fall's *Independent Democrat*.[12] In late August, the *El Paso Times* ran the following commentary on the situation:

> In New Mexico outlaws and murderers, upon whose heads a price has been set, are fond of being interviewed. . . . In the states an outlaw, dodging the officers of the law, would not think of writing letters to the press to excuse his crime. . . . But in New Mexico, Oliver Lee, after killing an officer of the law . . . sends the papers a graphic description of the fight he made and tells why he will not be arrested by this or that officer. And still some people wonder why New Mexico is not admitted to statehood.[13]

Lee claimed that Garrett never intended to arrest him at all, but to kill him. He said Garrett was brought in for the sole purpose of killing him.

Following the encounter with Garrett, Lee and Gililland likely spent much time at the ranch of Eugene Manlove Rhodes, who would go on to become a well-known writer. Life on the run didn't stop Oliver Lee from traveling to San Antonio, Texas, in October 1898 and marrying Winnie Rhode, the sister-in-law of W. W. Cox.[14]

It was early in 1899 when Albert Fall, finished with his military duty, returned to New Mexico.[15] Lee and Gililland were still in hiding. McNew was still in jail awaiting trial. While Fall began work to free McNew and help to get Lee and Gililland out of their situation, Governor Otero, working hard for statehood, continued to push to have this case solved and the killers brought to justice.

Otero was taking an active role in the case. Upon receiving information that a man in Yuma Penitentiary named Johnson, perhaps William Johnson, might have information regarding the Fountain case, the governor arranged a visit between him and Garrett. It was worked out beforehand between Otero and Arizona Territory Governor Nathan O. Murphy that if Otero got the information he wanted, Murphy would pardon Johnson.[16] Otero wrote in his biography many years later that Johnson told him, "I was with the party at some mining camp called Zunol [Sunol], or some such name." Otero said Johnson gave the names of several who were present, but Otero did not name them. Johnson went on to say, "they had a lookout who came in and reported that Fountain was on his way home and had stopped at Tularosa to rest. They hurriedly sent three men on horseback from the camp to where the road passes just north of the White Sands." Again, Otero wrote that Johnson mentioned these men by name, but Otero did not give the names. Johnson claimed that they showed him where the bodies were buried. He wanted a pardon before he would locate the bodies. Otero told him a pardon could only come after they were found, and talks broke off.[17]

It was just about this time that a new bill was being discussed in the New Mexico Legislature, one that was probably thought of by Albert Fall and one he certainly lobbied for. The bill was to create a new county from parts of Lincoln, Socorro, and Doña Ana counties. The purpose of the proposed new county was said to be to aid the building of a railroad passing through the area. A new county encompassing a smaller area would ensure business running more smoothly. The catch: The new county just barely included the site of Albert and Henry's murder. Thus, creation of this county would take jurisdiction away from Doña Ana County Sheriff Pat Garrett. Governor Otero at first opposed the proposal, but quickly changed his mind when Fall proposed that the new county be named Otero County. The bill passed and Otero appointed George Curry as Otero County's first sheriff.[18]

Now that the case was in the hands of Otero County and Lee's friend George Curry, Lee wrote to Governor Otero. It was worked out that he and Gilliland would surrender to Sheriff Curry and that they would never be incarcerated in the Las Cruces jail nor would they ever be in the custody of Pat Garrett. It should be noted that William McNew had been in Garrett's custody all this time and had not been harmed.

On March 13, 1899, Lee and Gilliland, with friend Eugene Rhodes, boarded a train at Aleman and headed south to Las Cruces to surrender. On that same train: Pat Garrett. Lee and Gilliland did not know Garrett was on the train when they boarded, yet they still traveled in disguise. Both men had heavy beards. Gilliland wore blue glasses and Lee wore a faded blue section hand's cap that was pulled down low. The last thing they wanted was to be arrested by Garrett while on their way to surrendering.

Garrett, aboard the train with friend and Texas Ranger Captain John Hughes, and a prisoner whom Hughes was taking back to Texas, walked through the train at every stop. At one point, Hughes and Garrett chained the prisoner to the day-coach seat and walked the train single file. They stopped in the smoking car, where Gilliland, Lee, and Rhodes sat. Garrett and Hughes stood without saying a word. Then they continued. That was their last walk through the train.

Did Pat Garrett recognize the fugitives? Rhodes and Lee thought he did not. Gililland believed that Garrett did but was too scared to arrest them. Hughes said afterward that he did not recognize them and believed that Garrett didn't either.

At Las Cruces, Lee, Gililland, and Rhodes left the train and walked by Deputy Ben Williams, who now knew about the arrangement and did nothing to stop it. They proceeded to the home of Judge Parker, where Parker and Curry waited. They surrendered to Parker and Curry took them into custody. Since the new jail for Otero County had not yet been built, Lee and Gililland were taken to Socorro to be held.[19]

Lee and Gililland were arraigned in Las Cruces. In that hearing Fall argued that the trial be moved to Otero County because Doña Ana County had no jurisdiction in the case. This was rejected. His argument that they could not receive a fair trial in Las Cruces was accepted.

The next hearing was held in Silver City with the case against William McNew being heard first. The prosecution requested a continuance, which the court rejected. The prosecution claimed that they didn't have the time and money to bring witnesses to Silver City for McNew's trial, but in reality, they did not want to show what they had in his trial before they could try Lee and Gililland, as they considered Lee the ringleader. Because of this, the prosecution dropped the charges against McNew for the murder of Albert Fountain. He was released, but still held under bond for the murder of Henry Fountain. It was decided that Lee and Gililland would be tried together for the murder of Henry Fountain. The Albert Fountain charge (and the Kearney charge) would be saved for later. The trial was set to begin on May 25, 1899, in the secluded mining town of Hillsboro.[20]

As the trial approached, Lee and Gililland were to be held in Socorro jail without bond. In reality, they were out much of the time, traveling to different towns and always willing to be interviewed. They were treated as celebrities.[21] In the meantime, the prosecution was gathering more evidence. They received a letter from a man named T. J. Daily. Daily said he was working for Oliver Lee at the time of the murders and claimed to be in "possession of facts that will bring about justice and to find the bodies." He said that he had not come forward with these facts sooner for fear he would be killed.[22] Three other witnesses also came forward. They claimed to have seen the murderers pass with the bodies of Albert and Henry. They had not come forward earlier on account of their own crime. They were stealing cattle at the time.[23]

James Gililland
(Date and photographer unknown.
Courtesy Palace of the Governors
[MNM/DCA], Negative No.
104696.)

thirteen

The Trial

Hillsboro was a mining town in the mountains in Sierra County with a population of only 1,000. It was a small desert town whose most impressive building was the Sierra County Courthouse, which sat on a hill. The nearest railroad was twenty miles south and the only public transportation into town were the stagecoach lines from the Nutt and Lake Valley train stations.

The Union Hotel was not nearly large enough to hold all of the people expected for the trial. As a result, tent towns were set up. The prosecution set up a camp at the north end of town with its own cook. The defense set up a camp that became known as "the Oliver Lee camp," at the south end of town. They had a chuck wagon to supply their food. Many friends and curious spectators who had come to town for the trial camped on the mountainsides.[1]

There was no telephone or telegraph in the secluded town. The Western Union Telegraph Company ran a line from Lake Valley to Hillsboro for the trial. Reporters were there from all of the area's newspapers as well as from many around the nation, the Associated Press, and the Hearst papers.[2]

Just after Albert Fall arrived in town, he took issue with another man who had arrived at the same time, prosecution witness and the colonel's son, Jack Fountain. Fall went before Judge Parker to plead for the safety of his clients and himself. He asked that Fountain be placed under a peace bond because of threats Fountain had made against them. Jack Fountain was brought before the bench.

Parker asked Fountain, "Is there any reason why this bond should not be imposed?"

Jack answered, "Your honor, I am just a young boy and have not had much experience, but I will say that I never said I intended to kill any of these men, and don't say so now, though they deserve killing. If the court pleases to hear me, I will state what I did say."

"You may make your statement."

"I said if my father's bones were ever found and identified, and I think I know how to identify them positively, there is one man I would kill first, if I were not killed myself."

"Who is that man?" Parker asked.

Jack pointed as he said, "Albert Bacon Fall." He was placed under a $500 bond.[3]

The murders Lee and Gililland were accused of quickly turned into an afterthought. The accused, along with their attorney Fall, became media darlings. The prisoners received flowers from sympathetic ladies. One eastern woman who attended the trial described Lee: "With quick eyes and unobtrusive manners, he carried himself as softly and easily as if he were at a tea party. I was amazed at his low voice and control, and a certain social grace." The same woman described Fall: "Slender, handsome in a gypsy way, he was brilliant, flashing, and most impressive."[4]

The big showdown finally came. Again, as in the McNew-Carr preliminaries, Republicans Richmond Barnes, William Childers, and Thomas Catron representing the prosecution faced Democrats Harvey Fergusson, Harry Daugherty, and Albert Fall for the defense.

Case No. 2618, Territory of New Mexico versus Oliver M. Lee and James R. Gililland, opened on May 26, 1899.[5]

When the indictment was read, charging the accused with the murder of Henry Fountain, Lee turned to his attorney Fergusson, aghast. "My God, Fergusson, they are not accusing me of the murder of a child." Lee and Gililland pled not guilty.[6]

William McNew sat near his friends. George Curry occupied a seat inside the rail. Lee took an active interest in the selection of the jurors, which took up the first two days.[7] The court appointed an interpreter because some of the jurors spoke only Spanish. Three had Spanish surnames.[8]

The prosecution faced some early problems. Several key witnesses were missing. Neither T. J. Daily, who worked at Lee's ranch at the time of the murder, or the three men who claimed to have seen the murderers with the bodies, appeared. The territory's expected first witness, Jack Maxwell, was not there either. It was claimed that he was missing due to illness. Pat Garrett left to hunt him down.[9] The prosecution must have hoped that Maxwell would fare better than he did at the McNew-Carr preliminary.

When jury selection finished, the prosecution asked for, and was granted, a continuance because their first witness had not arrived. The defense objected, but to no avail.[10]

Hillsboro, 1892. The courthouse is the big two-story building on a hill, left of center.
(Photograph by George T. Miller. Courtesy Palace of the Governors [MNM/DCA], Negative No. 76566.)

The testimony finally got underway on Monday morning, May 29. Maxwell was still not there, so the first witness called by the prosecution was former Governor William T. Thornton.

Thornton said, "I first heard of Colonel Fountain's death on the first Tuesday after it occurred." This immediately led to an objection. The defense insisted it be called a "disappearance," not "death."

Thornton continued, "I was informed that his buggy had been found and the supposition created that he had been murdered. I was requested to offer a reward and came to Las Cruces Tuesday night. Soon afterwards, Captain Van Patten gave me a package containing sand soaked with blood. I took it to Santa Fe where it was analyzed by a chemist and pronounced human blood. Later Captain Van Patten sent me a package of hair which had been shaved from the side of a white horse. This was also saturated with blood and was analyzed."

Albert Fall cross-examined Thornton. "Who sent for you to go to Las Cruces?" Fall asked.

"I think Llewellyn and Numa Reymond asked me to offer a reward, but I don't know whether they asked me to come to Cruces or not."

"Didn't you receive a telegram from Thomas Tucker asking you to come?"

"No sir, I think not."

"Didn't you state there that you had received a telegram from Tucker?"

"No sir. I am certain Tucker never sent me any telegram."[11]

Antonio Garcia was the next to testify. The *El Paso Herald* noted, "He is an aged Mexican and it was necessary for the court interpreter to work hard during the examination."

Garcia told the court that he saw Henry and Colonel Fountain the day they started for Lincoln, and again the next day near Parker's Well when he and Albert Fountain went there with the colonel's horses that had run off. Garcia was next asked about and went on to detail the search. He said that the posse he joined to look for Henry Fountain and his father "went east from Las Cruces toward the Chalk Hills and stayed all night near the lakes." Their posse met the other search party the next morning.

He then told of finding Colonel Fountain's buckboard, with a number of boot tracks around it. He said a portion of the posse remained with the buckboard while others followed the trail of horses. "There were tracks of six horses leading away from the vehicle in a bunch. We followed them to the hills, where they separated. We followed one of the trails made by three of the horses across the Jarillas toward the Sacramentos, and about six miles from the Sacramentos the trail was obliterated and lost by the crossing of a herd of cattle." At that point, the searching party abandoned the trail and went to Wildy Well to get water.

Fall then got his chance to cross-examine, and he tore into the old man. He began by asking him about going with Albert Fountain to bring the colonel's horses back to him at Parker's Well, then moved on to the search for the Fountains.

"How did you first find the trail of Colonel Fountain's buckboard?"

"It was shown to me by the boy at the stage station."

"Did you not testify this morning that it was no trouble for you to find the buggy tracks, as there had been no other tracks made there?"

"It was the only vehicle track on the road."

"Then how did the mail rider get over the road with his vehicle after Colonel Fountain passed?" Fall asked the old man.

"I do not know."

Fall moved on to question Garcia about finding Fountain's buckboard, and what was there. Fall asked him, "Did you see any tracks there that you noticed were the little boy's?"

"I don't remember."

"Who was the first man to reach the buckboard?"

"I don't remember."

"After you met Major Llewellyn, you say you and the trailer rode ahead. How far ahead?"

"I can't calculate the distance."

"When Major Llewellyn left, what direction did he take?"

"He went toward the Dog Canyon."

"Did he go off to your right or to your left?"

"He went in front."

"Were you going toward Dog Canyon?"

"No sir."

"Then if he went off in front of you he couldn't have been going towards Dog Canyon, could he?"

Garcia seemed embarrassed as he answered, "No."

The *Herald* reported, "The witness was then subjected to a long and laborious cross examination concerning locations, distances and directions and he was badly tangled up by Judge Fall, who appeared to be perfectly familiar with the country to the east of Las Cruces."

Childers stepped back up for the prosecution. He asked Garcia, "Was your party riding single or double file while traveling?"

"Single file."

"Did you see any other cattle besides that herd you spoke about?"

"Yes, we could see animals in all directions."

"Did you see any loose horses near the trail?"

"No, not near, but in sight, long way off."[12]

After lunch, Albert Fountain took the stand. Fountain, after being sworn in, stated that he lived in Mesilla and was the son of Colonel Albert J. Fountain. He said that he last saw his father when he, along with his father-in-law Garcia, brought the colonel's horses to him.

Fountain testified that he first heard of his father's disappearance when Barela arrived and told what he had seen. Fountain left Mesilla with a posse upon hearing the news. They stopped at Parker's Well, and then went to Luna's Well, where they learned that his father and Henry had passed through on their way to Las Cruces.

He said that they trailed the colonel's buckboard towards Chalk Hill and near that point, behind a green bush, a few feet from the road where the buckboard passed, were tracks and imprints in the sand, as if a man had sat behind a bush. He said that the tracks were apparently made by cowboy boots. The tracks showed that the buckboard and three horsemen left the road. "The horse that had been tied behind the vehicle in passing the bush apparently ran around to the other side of the buckboard as if frightened. There were tracks of men and horses around the spot. We followed the trail through the cut and some distance further on saw where the buggy and horse had stopped in the road. We knew they had stopped by the tracks of the horses, for they had stamped their feet, as if restless. A number of cigarette papers were scattered around on the ground." He said the buckboard was about five miles from the road.

"Further on we met the other searching party, who reported having found the dismantled buggy, and we accompanied them to the spot where it was standing. The valise and boxes had been opened and their contents were either missing or scattered around. The little hat of Henry's had been left behind inside the valise. A bottle of liquor had been broken. The tracks of three men were plainly visible in the sand at and around the vehicle and the horse tracks led away from it straight toward the Jarillas."

He said the tracks of six horses were visible. They followed the trail of the horses five miles, and there found "the charred remnants of a campfire, where the parties had apparently spent the night." Around the campfire "were tracks of several men, one wearing box-toed shoes and the other narrow, and the track of a child of about eight years of age."

He continued, "We discovered where the trail of one horse branched off from the rest and took a zigzag course as if unwilling to leave the bunch. The tracks of the single horse were identified as those of Colonel Fountain's little mare." They followed the trail toward the Jarilla Mountains. At the point of the Jarilla Mountains, another horse left the party and headed towards the pass near the southern end of the Jarillas. Albert's party did not follow that trail, but the main trail, which crossed the Jarillas and went east towards the Sacramentos. As they reached the west slope of the Sacramentos, the trail was obliterated by a herd of cattle and lost.

A map of the country was produced and Fountain pointed out the various places visited by the searching party and the spot where the buckboard was found. He said Major Llewellyn had measured the tracks at the campsite with a pocket ruler. He also said that there was no doubt that there was a boy's tracks among them, but he could not swear as to whether the tracks were made with shoes belonging to one or both feet.

Harry Daugherty cross-examined the witness. He first questioned Albert about his father's horses being stampeded off on his first night away from Mesilla. He asked what stampeded the horses.

Albert responded, "A wild animal of some kind."

"Did you find any evidence of anyone being camped near?"

"Yes, there was a man camped not far from my father."

Daugherty went on to ask, "The country south of Luna's Wells is of a rough contour, is it not?"

"Yes sir."

"How far from the road could you see a horseman?"

The prosecution objected. It was sustained.

Daugherty continued. "At the buckboard, Mr. Fountain, you say that most of the clothing of the little boy was gone?"

"The coat was gone."

The redirect was done by Childers. He asked Fountain, "What kind of clothing was left behind at the buckboard?"

"An old suit of my father's and the little boy's coat and hat and two shawls. My father's cartridge belt was also found on the seat of the buggy, but his rifle was gone." Fountain was excused.[13]

The next morning, Theodore Herman took the stand. He was the foreman of the Lincoln County grand jury in 1896 that had indicted Lee and McNew. Herman said that indictments were found against Lee and McNew for larceny of cattle, and that these indictments had been obtained chiefly through the efforts of Colonel Fountain. The defense attorneys objected strenuously to the introduction of this evidence, as it showed a motive for the alleged crime. Parker overruled the objection. Certified copies of the indictments were brought before the jury. On cross-examination, the witness did say that Les Dow was the chief witness against Lee and McNew. It was on Dow's testimony that the indictments were brought.[14]

Saturnino Barela was the next witness called. He repeated his often told story of seeing three horsemen outlined against the sky; his conversation with Fountain; the buggy tracks leaving the road the next day. "I followed the trail afoot some yards after it left the road and noticed the tracks of another horse. I then went back to my buggy and drove to Las Cruces and reported to Albert Fountain my fears and what I had seen. I first asked for Colonel Fountain and they told me he hadn't arrived."

His story did not change on cross-examination.[15]

Catarino Villegas, a member of the search party, was called next. He corroborated the testimony of Albert Fountain and Antonio Garcia about what the searching party found. He said he was with the posse led by Major Llewellyn that followed the trail that was obliterated by a man driving a herd of cattle across it.

During the cross-examination, Villegas was asked, "How many of you got off your horses at the buckboard?"

"Two of us."

"Did you walk round the buckboard?"

"Yes."

"You found some shawls there, didn't you?"

"Yes."

"Did you take them back to Mr. Fountain and show them to him?"

"No sir."

"Did you ride all round the buckboard?"

"We went all round it on foot."

"Are you positive of this?"

"Yes."

"And you saw there three tracks, so that you could distinguish the difference between them?"

"Yes."

"You say that the horses which went over the pass were not shod?"

"I don't know."

"Who was the trailer?"

"I was one of them."

"You were one of the trailers and yet didn't pay enough attention to know whether the horses were shod or not?"

Villegas response was not recorded.[16]

Major Eugene Van Patten was called to the stand. Van Patten stated that he was living in Las Cruces in 1896 and was acquainted with the Fountains at the time of their disappearance. He went out with a search party to look for them.

When asked what he found, Van Patten said, "Among other things, I found a pool of blood on the ground 424 paces south of Chalk Hill on the main road near where Fountain's buckboard left the road. I also found a five and a ten-cent piece. The pool of blood was in one of the roads of the cutoff. It was seven or eight inches deep and twice or three times as large as a spittoon," he said, pointing to a courtroom cuspidor. "The blood had spattered around for a distance of six feet. The pool looked as if a blanket had been drawn through one side—"

"Hold on there!" exclaimed the three defense attorneys in unison, cutting off Van Patten. "Don't go any further," said one of the attorneys for the defense. "That kind of evidence is not admissible."

"Gentlemen," Judge Parker said dryly, "if you have any objections to make, make them to the court. That mode of procedure will not be tolerated longer."

"We understand, your honor," said Fall, "and intend to make them to the court, but our intention was to stop this ready witness before he could place incompetent evidence before the jury." Parker agreed with the objection and ruled out the testimony concerning the blanket.

Van Patten continued. A map was shown to the jury to aid him in telling his story. "Near the buckboard I found several human tracks and prints of knees behind a bush and several empty shells."

He said he followed the trail of the horses and the trail led him through a camp "occupied by several men." He would go on to find Fountain's gray horse.

"Did you examine carefully the trail of the buckboard leading from the Chalk Hill?"

"I did sir; it showed that there were three horses. Two pulling the vehicle and one tethered behind it."

Van Patten said the horses that overtook the buckboard were trotting after surrounding it.

"Did Colonel Fountain have a Winchester?"

"When he left Las Cruces he did. It was either 44 or 40 caliber."

"Did you go back to this spot where the blood was found?"

"I did, and I got up some of the sand and gave it to Governor Thornton. I had some of the hair from the side of the gray horse shaved off and sent it to Governor Thornton. It was soaked with blood."

"What was the condition of that gray horse when you found him?"

"He was jaded and had bloodstains on him. The stains were on his left side below the saddle. The horse had [a] sore back, but it was not a bleeding sore."

"Did you see any indications of anybody having been on the ground near the pool of blood?"

The defense objected and it was sustained. Fall got up to cross-examine the witness. "You testified in the preliminary hearing of McNew, didn't you?"

"Yes sir," Van Patten answered.

"You haven't repeated it to the jury as you told it there, have you?"

"I've told it as near as I could about what happened."

Fall walked up to Van Patten, stood directly in front of him, and interrogated him sharply concerning his former testimony at the McNew-Carr hearing. When Van Patten said that he did not say a certain fact, Fall read from the transcript and asked the witness if he did not testify that he trailed the gray horse east from the pool of blood then north.

"I testified that then and now," Van Patten responded. He gave similar answers to other questions of the like. The interrogation continued until Van Patten finally said, in answer to one of Fall's questions, "I might have been mixed up then just like you are trying to mix me up now."

"I don't want you to mix up at all," Fall replied. "I want to unmix you."

A short time later, Fall asked him what time he found the blood. Van Patten said it was the tenth of the month.

"Did you find a jack rabbit that had been recently killed there and what you claim were the brains of the child near the pool of blood?"

"I did not."

"It was either the 10th or 11th then that you found this blood. Now, who did you send it in town by, or did you take it yourself?"

"I took it myself."

"Who found the gray horse?"

"I was with the men who found him."

"Albert Fountain testified there was no blood on that horse, then he was mistaken?"

The prosecution objected, saying that Fountain had given no such testimony in the present trial, and that the evidence of the McNew preliminary had nothing to do with the case on trial.

Fall turned to the clerk. "Mr. Clerk, issue a subpoena for Albert Fountain and we will hold him as a witness for the defense." The subpoena was issued and served. Van Patten was then excused, with the defense reserving the right to call him later. It was decided that the court would not hold a session that night and court adjourned for the day.[17]

Sierra County Courthouse, 1892. Shortly after this photograph was taken, a jail was built behind the courthouse. (Photograph by George T. Miller. Courtesy of Palace of the Governors [MNM/DCA], Negative No. 76564.)

Remains of the Sierra County Courthouse, 2006. The jail can be seen behind the courthouse. (Author's photograph)

fourteen

Jack Maxwell Testifies

The next day led off with the witness whom the prosecution had been waiting for. Jack Maxwell, who claimed he had been absent due to illness, was brought into town by Ben Williams. Maxwell was finally sworn in and took the stand.

Maxwell stated that he had known Lee and Gililland for five or six years and that his ranch was not very far from Lee's. "On February 1, 1896, I was at Dog Canyon ranch and spent the night there. I got there just before sundown. When I got there I found Mrs. Lee [Oilver's mother], Mr. Blevins, Mr. Bailey, and Ed, the colored man. I ate supper there that night and slept in the house with Mr. Blevins."

"What time did you get up Sunday morning?" Childers asked.

"At sunup and I ate breakfast with Mr. Blevins and others."

"Did you see either of these defendants there for breakfast?"

"No sir."

"What did you do that day?"

"I stayed down at the corral."

To an unknown question, Maxwell answered, "Saw four persons mounted on two horses coming from the northeast toward the house. They came within 200 yards from me and dismounted."

"Who were these people?"

"I took them to be Mr. Lee, Mr. Gililland, Mr. McNew, and Negro Ed."

Maxwell testified, "I ate dinner there that day with Lee, McNew, and Gililland and supper that night. I think Mr. Blevins was not there at dinner, but returned to supper." He answered another question, "I slept that night with McNew. Lee and Gililland took their bedding and went outside to sleep. They had their ordinary arms with them."

Maxwell later said that his horse and two others were in Lee's corral. "The two belonged to the ranch, I think. . . . Those were the two horses which the four men rode up to the ranch on. I do not know what time the horses left the ranch. . . . Tuesday morning I went to the pasture, a mile from the house, to get my horse. There were five or six other horses there, but I disremember exactly. The other horses looked like they had been used lately and had been used hard."

"Did some of them attract your attention more than others?" Maxwell was asked.

"I don't know that they did," he responded. "I think there was two roan [brownish coat sprinkled with white or gray] horses and one bay in the bunch. All the horses looked like they had been rode, judging from the sweat marks and saddle marks, but I can't say how much."

"Did you not testify in the McNew preliminary before Judge Parker at Las Cruces?"

"Yes sir."

"Did you not then testify as follows?" and Childers began to read from the transcript. Fall immediately objected, but it was overruled.

"Well," Childers began, "you testified before that two of the horses had been ridden harder than the others. Which horses were those?"

"I don't remember." That response quickly became common for Maxwell, as he had forgotten many points that he had testified to at the McNew-Carr preliminary hearing. The prosecution proved unsuccessful in attempting to bring out evidence about the jaded horses, and the defense objected to the prosecution's reading from the transcript, alleging that they were trying to contradict their own witness.

Albert Fall cross-examined the witness. "Mr. Maxwell, when you testified at the preliminary examination, you testified practically the same things about going to Lee's ranch that you have now, except as to dates?"

"Yes sir."

"When you left Las Cruces after the preliminary, where did you go?"

"I left there on the train for Colorado Springs and went to work for the Alpine Cattle Company. I left Las Cruces on the train with Mr. Childers. He paid for my fare and got me a job."

"Did Mr. Childers say anything to you about your life being in danger if you went back to Otero County? Did you not tell Bud Smith after you got back that Mr. Childers had told you you had better go away as defendants or their friends would kill you?"

This was objected to by the prosecution and overruled.

"Yes," said Maxwell.

"You were at Silver City when the McNew case was called," Fall said. "Did you have any conversation about these horses with Mr. Childers?"

"No sir."

"Did you have any conversation with Mr. Childers last night after you got here?"

"Yes sir."

"Did he tell you what he would do to you if you failed to testify?"

"No sir."

"What time was it you said you got into Dog Canyon ranch?"

"Just about nine."

"And you got back on Tuesday?"

"Yes sir."

"When did you hear of the disappearance of Colonel Fountain?"

"I disremember."

"Did you not tell Bud Smith within a week after February 1, 1896, they need not accuse Oliver Lee or any of these boys of the murder of Colonel Fountain for you were there and saw Lee setting out grapevines with Mrs. Lee and the other boys were also there at work?"

"I didn't state it that way."

"Did you not state to this man that Oliver Lee and the other men were at the ranch on Saturday, and you knew they had nothing to do with Fountain's murder?"

"No sir."

"Did you tell George Curry that you were at Dog Canyon ranch Saturday afternoon and that Lee and Gililland were there?"

"I didn't tell anyone that I was there in the afternoon."

"Is it not a fact that this is the first time that you have been able to fix the day of the week when you got to Dog Canyon, or when you left there, or the day of the month?"

"I hadn't thought of the day of the month before I got back to Tularosa and heard of Fountain's disappearance."

"Then you were mistaken when you said that you waited until the mail came in before you heard about Fountain?"

"I heard about it in Tularosa."

Fall then read back Maxwell's testimony from the preliminary, where Maxwell said that he thought he went to the ranch on Saturday, but was not certain as to whether it was January or February and couldn't fix the date. Maxwell admitted that he had then said that.

Fall continued the questioning, "Didn't you write a letter to Jack Tucker telling him that you would make a good witness for the boys as you could swear that they were forty miles away when Fountain disappeared?"

Maxwell then denied having made any such statement, but admitted to having written a letter to Tucker.

Fall moved on. "Has anyone ever promised you any remuneration for the evidence you should give in this case?"

"Any what?"

"Any pay," said Judge Parker.

"No," replied Maxwell in what was described as an injured tone.

"Is it not a fact that you were made a written contract with Pat Garrett?"

"Yes sir."

"Is it not a fact that the contract was signed by Pat Garrett and Charles Perry and reads substantially as follows: 'We the undersigned agree to pay J. W. Maxwell $2000 for evidence leading to the conviction of the Fountain murderers. Said $2000 to be paid upon conviction.'"

"I don't know that these were the words," Maxwell responded. "I was to get $2000 of the reward."

"What were you to do for that $2000?" Fall asked, in his attempt to make a common reward look like a bribe.

"Simply to tell the plain facts of what I knew about this case."

"Isn't it a fact that you told Pat Garrett and Mr. Perry that you knew certain facts and would not swear to them until they had given you $2000?"

"They gave me the contract before I told them what I knew."

"If Garrett says to the contrary, then he tells an untruth, does he not?"

Objected to by the prosecution and sustained.

"Mr. Maxwell," Fall said, "before you got this contract did not Mr. Charles Perry tell you that you would have to do something to clear yourself?"

"No, he didn't tell me in that way."

"Didn't you tell me that Mr. Perry told you that unless you

gave evidence convicting these men you might be hung yourself?"

"No sir."

Fall changed the line of questioning. "Where were you born?" he asked.

"In Alabama."

Then, in answers to various questions, Maxwell stated he had lived in Mississippi, in Texas for six years, and from there he went to Colorado, where he only stayed for a short time. He moved to Doña Ana County, where he went by the name of Jack Maxwell. When living in the Texas Panhandle, he went by the name of J. B. Alexander. Fall asked him, "Why did you change your name when you went to No Man's Land?"

"I was ashamed to let people know I had ever been in that strip." The response brought laughter to the courtroom.

"Is it not a fact that you stated to Bud Smith, at some time before the examination of McNew, that at the trial of Pat Saunders you swore to a lie?"

"No sir," he answered indignantly.

"Did you have any conversation with George Swaggart about this contract?"

"I don't remember ever having any."

"Didn't you tell him that you had a contract for $2000 for your evidence in this case and that you wanted the money and didn't give a damn how you got it?"

"No sir." Then came the noon recess.

After recess, Fall continued his questioning of Maxwell. "Did you have the following conversation in October, 1897, with Captain Curry at Tularosa, and tell him that your evidence would clear Lee; that you slept with Lee that night?"

"No sir."

After a few more questions, Childers got up for the redirect. "What did you tell us at Las Cruces the night before you testified?"

"I told you I was too full to testify," Maxwell replied.

"Didn't you tell us that it would be as much as your life was worth to testify against these men?"

"I didn't tell it just in that way. I told you that I owned a homestead in that country and that I did not want to go on the stand and testify while I was drunk for fear I would make misstatements that might cause me further trouble."

"Has anybody connected with the prosecution of this case ever asked you to state anything except what was the truth, except what you knew?"

"No sir."

"Did you receive anything from me when you went to Colorado City except money to pay your traveling expenses and a letter to the foreman?"

"No sir."

"You just earned wages on that ranch like anybody else, did you not?"

"Yes sir."

Fall re-cross-examined the witness. "The fact of it is you were not frightened by these defendants at all, were you?"

"I don't know what it is to be frightened," Maxwell said, with emphasis on the "I." The courtroom filled with laughter. Maxwell was excused.[1]

Mail carrier Santos Alvarado followed Maxwell to the stand. Alvarado testified that he had met Colonel Fountain on the road between Tularosa and Luna's Well, February 1, 1896. Before seeing the Fountain vehicle, Santos saw two horsemen. They seemed to be traveling toward the Sacramentos, coming from the Tularosa-La Luz vicinity. He started off toward the horsemen and they took off in a gallop. He later met Fountain and told him about the horsemen.[2]

Barela was recalled briefly, followed by the colonel's son Albert.

On cross-examination, Fall asked Fountain about the "white horse" and the supposed blood on its side. It was reported as questions about the white horse, but it was the same horse that Van Patten called gray and Thornton white in earlier testimony. The witness said the white horse had a sore back and had been sweating considerably. It also seemed that something wide had been thrown on its back, like a blanket, causing it to sweat and its side to be dyed from the cloth. "I did not find any blood on the horse," Albert stated. He said when he saw the horse that the hair had already been shaved off.[3]

Albert's younger brother Jack was the next witness to take the stand. He stated that he last saw his father and brother Henry in January 1896, at the Mescalero Indian Agency (Blazer's Mill) on their way to court in Lincoln.

"I was in Cruces when word came that my father's vehicle had been taken off the road." Jack Fountain went on to tell of the search by the party that immediately left Las Cruces. His testimony was much the same as the others in that search party.

"Near the Chalk Hills the tracks of three horsemen overtook the buggy," he said. "One seemed to pass along on either side of the road at the head of the horses, and the third followed. They turned directly off the road to the east toward the Jarillas, taking the vehicle with them."

Jack described following the tracks to the buckboard, and to the remnants of a campfire five miles beyond. He said he saw the tracks of three men and the same three horses around the fire but saw no tracks of a child. He followed the trail until a herd of cattle "crossed the trail and obliterated it seven miles from Lee's wells."

Jack Fountain was cross-examined by Albert Fall. He said the gray horse was shod by Antonio Garcia, who reduced an old set of large shoes to fit the horse's feet and he failed to put heels on them, so the tracks of this horse were easy to distinguish.

Fall pulled out a copy of the *Rio Grande Republican's* "Extra" edition, published shortly after the Fountain disappearance. In an interview to the paper, Jack Fountain was quoted as saying that he had seen both his father's and brother's footprints in the sand near the buckboard. Fountain said he was misquoted and categorically denied ever making such a statement.[4]

The first witness of that night's session was Nicholas Armijo. Armijo testified that he was a member of one of the searching parties that went out on news of Fountain's disappearance. He aided in trailing the buckboard and saw the pool of blood on the ground. On cross-examination, it took Armijo, a mountain man, fully ten minutes to remember the present month and year, and he did not know the day of the week.[5]

David H. Sutherland was the next to take the stand. Sutherland last saw Colonel Fountain on February 1, 1896. Fountain arrived at Sutherland's home in La Luz the previous day, traveling by buckboard. Fountain left in the morning after having spent the night there. Sutherland stated that Fountain had a rifle and cartridge belts, two Navajo blankets, a small wooden box, thirty inches of rope, a telescope valise, and a small bunch of baled alfalfa. He said Fountain left his house between seven and eight o'clock and that he was wearing wide-soled shoes.

On cross-examination, Fall asked Sutherland, "Are you a friend of Mr. Lee's?"

"Not particularly, no."

"Had a personal difficulty with him several years ago, did you not?"

"Yes sir."

"Since that time you have not been at all friendly, have you?"

"No sir."[6]

fifteen

Garrett Takes the Stand

The next morning, James Gould, whose cousin was Gililland's wife, took the stand. The witness stated that he was at McNew's ranch about the first of February 1896. Gililland had come in a few days before, changed horses, got some cartridges, and left. When he returned, he was accompanied by McNew. Gould said they had told him about Fountain's disappearance, which was the first he had heard of it.

Gould also said, "Gililland said a posse was out hunting for Fountain and at dinner at Lee's ranch young Fountain had become frightened and jumped up and seized his gun. Fountain was eating dinner there and had a fit, vowing vengeance on the murderers of his father."

Gould testified to a conversation he had had while working on a fence with Gililland when Gililland "told me that old man Fountain had come from Texas in a chicken coop and prized up [pried up] hell ever since he had been in New Mexico, but he wouldn't prize up anymore. I asked him how about killing the child and he said, 'the child was nothing but a half breed and to kill him was like killing a dog.'"

Fall cross-examined the witness. "What was the date of this last conversation?"

"I don't know exactly. Must have been along in the latter part of February."

"Who was present?"

"No one was present except myself."

"You testified in this case before, didn't you?"

"Yes sir."

"You forgot to tell about that conversation before, didn't you?"

"No, I don't know that I did."

"You've talked this story over with your father, haven't you, and are trying to tell part of his story and part of yours?"

"I don't know that I am."

Fall went on to ask him, "Where were you in March 1897?"

"I was in the Eddy jail."

Fall later asked, "Are you a friend or enemy of Mr. Gililland?"

"An enemy I suppose, now," Gould responded.

"How about Mr. McNew?"

"Well, Mr. McNew don't speak to me."

"For a long time prior to the arrest of McNew at Las Cruces all you parties up there in the Sacramentos were going armed for one another and were expecting trouble, were you not?"

"We carried pistols."

"The fact of the matter was you and your father and Kearney expected McNew and others to attack you, didn't you?"

"I was afraid they were going to attack me, but didn't know about the rest."

"Has there been any threatened trouble between your people and Gililland's friends?"

"Don't know of any threats."

"Were you not at all well armed?"

"Yes, we thought Gililland might raise trouble with me and carried firearms some time before McNew's preliminary hearing."[1]

Riley Baker was called. He and James Gililland were married to sisters. Baker testified that he knew Colonel Fountain and became acquainted with Gililland after the disappearance. Baker had to be asked to look the jury in the face, but continued to keep his eyes roving the floor.

He said Gililland showed him the point where he, Lee, and McNew watched the search party with a pair of field glasses. "Afterwards, while we were riding through the Sacramentos, I told Gililland I didn't know who murdered the Fountains, but the murder of the child was a mighty low down thing. Gililland said, oh, he didn't know, 'as the child was no better than a dog.'"

Gililland told Baker, in the presence of Kent Kearney, that the bodies would never be found and no one would be convicted for the murder. "Gililland said things had been more quiet since the old man was missing—or killed—I don't know which."

During cross examination by Fall, Baker admitted to waiting on top of a house in Alamogordo on election day in the hopes of arresting Lee and Gililland when they came to vote. Baker said he was up there with his brother, son, and H. W. Loomis. It was Deputy Sheriff Loomis who had told them to get on the house to wait for Lee.

"Did you have a warrant for Lee?" Fall asked.

"Yes sir."

On the re-cross-examination, Fall asked Baker, "Did you ever receive any pay for your services as deputy sheriff?"

"Yes sir, several times. I was to get $1.50 per day for watching on the house at Alamogordo."

"Were you to get any more for killing Lee?" Fall asked in his typical fashion just to get the idea in the minds of the jury.

"There was nothing said about killing Lee." Baker was excused.[2]

Humphrey Hill was called next. Hill had seen Fountain on January 31, 1896. The prosecution asked Hill questions about a conversation he had had with Fountain when they met on the road. "Had Colonel Fountain any apprehension of danger at the hands of parties who were following him?"

Objected to and overruled.

"He said that he was afraid. He told me that he had been up there getting indictments against certain parties and he was afraid of these parties."

Fountain told Hill that three horsemen were following him. The defense objected on the grounds that the evidence was hearsay, alleging the witness was testifying about what Fountain had said about information given to him by a third party. The jury was excused and an argument between the attorneys followed, lasting a full hour. The court finally ruled that it was "clearly incompetent to establish any fact by the witness which was not stated to him by Colonel Fountain out of his own mouth. If, however, a conspiracy had been shown among the three men to murder Fountain then the evidence was competent." Hill was withdrawn but held for later testimony.[3]

James W. Gould Sr. was called next. The witness stated that he was acquainted with Lee and Gililland and in 1896 lived in the locality where Fountain disappeared.

He testified to a conversation he had had with Gililland during which Gililland said that, "it made no difference about the boy as he was only a half breed," and, "that things had been very quiet since Fountain disappeared."

On cross-examination, Fall asked Gould if he was the same James Gould who had been tried, convicted, and sent to the penitentiary for three years for the theft of bacon in 1878. Gould admitted that he was.

Fall soon after asked, "You have been an enemy of McNew for years, haven't you?"

"No sir."

"On a trip up to El Paso you said that you would kill that son of a bitch McNew and your brother would swear out of it? That you would kill Gililland if he did not quit running with McNew?"

"No sir."[4]

The next witness, Frank Wayne, who lived in the Sacramentos twenty-five miles from Lee's ranch, said he was at Lee's Dog Canyon ranch before or about February 1, 1896, looking for a pony.

"When I left there, Mr. Lee rode out with my brother about two miles," said Wayne. "When he went to start back he said, 'You boys say nothing about what you saw here, as it might interfere with some of our plans.'"

Wayne was not cross-examined.[5]

Charles S. Lusk testified next. Lusk, while a deputy sheriff, took McNew to Las Cruces in January 1896, where he gave bond to appear and answer to an indictment found against him at the January term. Lusk said that on the streets of Las Cruces McNew told him that while Fountain had no hopes of gaining a conviction against him and the other indicted persons, he intended to prosecute them anyway in order to break them apart.

Fall objected on the grounds that McNew was not on trial. The prosecution argued that there was a conspiracy and that all the defendants stood together. The objection was sustained.

After testifying that he attended court in Lincoln where Fountain prosecuted alleged cattle thieves, Lusk was excused.[6] Pat Garrett's name was called next. A hush fell over the crowd as the tall sheriff entered the room. Heads turned and there was a murmur among the spectators as Garrett walked down the aisle and took the stand. The crowd would not be disappointed.

Sheriff Garrett stated that he resided in Las Cruces and was currently the sheriff of Doña Ana County. He said that he had lived in Texas and did not become acquainted with the defendants until he moved to New Mexico in 1896. He also knew Colonel Fountain from his earlier days in New Mexico.

Garrett said that he visited Chalk Hill in March 1896 to investigate the disappearance. Major Van Patten, E. E. Banner, and others were with him. He said he "found blood where the supposed murder of Colonel Fountain took place," and he "judged that a man had been killed there." The sheriff said, "The pool was probably 12 to 15 inches across."

Garrett was asked about his efforts to bring in Lee and Gililland. "I had a warrant for Lee and Gililland in 1898 and made several efforts to serve it, but they objected. I got the two together at one time, but they resisted and killed Kearney, my deputy. I made several other scouting trips into the mountains but failed to find the defendants. I also sent various other parties out to look for the defendants, H. W. Loomis, Riley Baker, and others."

He was questioned about the encounter at Wildy Well.

Garrett said they did not find the two in the house, but discovered them on the roof.

"After making several efforts to get word to them to surrender I told the boys that we would have to crawl up there by means of a ladder and call on them to surrender."

"Mr. Lee and Mr. Kearney shot at about the same time, but Mr. Kearney shot first and Mr. Kearney was mortally wounded."

Garrett was asked about Jack Maxwell and the reward promised to him.

"I made a written contract with him to furnish the evidence for the conviction of the Fountain murderers." Garrett produced a copy of the original contract, which was presented to the jury.

The next morning, Albert Fall began his cross-examination of Garrett.

Garrett said he was paid $300 monthly for his services prior to the time he became sheriff.

"You held a conference in El Paso with whom?" Fall asked.

"Llewellyn, Jim Beard, and others."

"Was evidence which they purported to have in the Fountain case then given to you?"

"Yes sir. They gave me evidence tending to implicate Lee, Gililland, McNew, and an official of Doña Ana." Most everyone in the courtroom must have been aware of the official Garrett referred to. Garrett told of having persuaded Fall to visit Santa Fe to have him appointed sheriff. The visit resulted in the discharge of two county commissioners and Garrett was then appointed.

"Did you ever at any time while Sheriff of Doña Ana County have any conversation with Mr. Lee relative that if warrants were issued for him he was to surrender?"

"Not that I know of."

"Do you remember of telling Mr. Lee not to surrender to any posse of which Ben Williams was a member?"

"No sir, but I told him I thought it would be unwise," Garrett replied.

"What was the condition of affairs when you first went to Las Cruces?"

"Well, you fellows had been shooting at one another and cutting up."

"What fellows?"

"You and Lee and Williams and others."

"Didn't you tell me that Williams had a mania for killing?"

Objected and sustained.

"At the time you went to Las Cruces political feeling was running pretty high, wasn't it?"

"That's what they called it."

The prosecution objected to the witness being examined on politics. It was sustained.

"What was Lee's official position when you went into Doña Ana County?"

"I understood he was a Deputy Sheriff."

Fall asked for and was granted permission to question Garrett as to his opinion of Williams for the reason that Williams was afterwards a member of a posse that went after the defendants.

"Is it not a fact that Ben Williams was a maniac on the subject of killing?"

"I told you he was a maniac not to murder, but on the subject of killing."

"What did you say would be your course if given any warrants for the arrest of Lee? Did you not say that you would go after him by yourself?"

"Yes sir."

"Upon what were these warrants based?"

"Upon affidavits."

"They were issued four terms after Fountain disappeared, were they not, and after the grand jury adjourned?"

"Yes sir."

"Who made the affidavit before warrants for defendants were issued?"

"I did," Garrett stated.

"At that time you knew what Jack Fountain and other witnesses would testify, did you not?"

Objected to. Fall argued the admissibility of the evidence, as he attempted to show that the prosecution had all of its evidence two years before Lee was indicted. The objection was sustained.

Fall asked Garrett, "When this evidence came into your hands, why did you not apply for a bench warrant?"

"I didn't think it was the proper time."

"Why didn't you think it was the proper time?"

"You had too much control of the courts down there." Garrett's answer caused much laughter.

"In other words, you thought I was the administration?"

"You came pretty near it."

"You base your conclusions on the fact that I procured the sheriff's office for you?"

"Well, you showed your strength then."

"What did you do when these warrants were sworn out?"

"Sent out a posse to serve them."

"Isn't it a fact that this posse was composed of members of Major,

Captain, or General Van Patten's militia, and that they pressed food from citizens on the grounds that they were militia men?"

"Not to my knowledge."

"What was your object in sending this mob after Lee and Gililland?"

"It was not a mob, it was a posse."

"Was John Meadows in the party?"

"Yes sir."

"You know his record. Was he ever sent to the penitentiary?"

"I don't know anything about it, but I am satisfied he wasn't." Meadows would later be asked similar questions about his past.

Fall continued to inquire about Meadows, asking, "What name did he go under when you first knew him?"

"John Gray."

Garrett was asked about the visit made by his posse to Lee's Wildy Well ranch. He was asked to show, by means of a diagram, the house on which Lee and Gililland slept and the shed roof close by on which some of the posse climbed.

Fall asked him, "You say when you climbed up on the roof you hallooed, 'Surrender' or 'throw up your hands'?"

"Kearney and I both hallooed it."

"Could you see Lee and was he armed?"

"Yes, I could see him and his gun."

"Didn't you tell me afterwards that Kearney fired too quick and contrary to the orders you had given him?"

"I told you I thought he fired too quick."

"What took place then?"

"I fired a few shots myself, and it got to be a general skirmish. I fired two shots."

"Then what did you do?"

"I went to Kearney and assisted him off the roof."

"We had a little conversation with Lee. He said, 'You are a hell of a lot of fellows to order a man to throw up his hands and shoot at the same time.' I told him that I thought Kearney had shot a little too quick. We talked a while about Lee surrendering. He said he didn't believe he would surrender to me as he had heard that I had said that I intended killing him. I assured him he would be perfectly safe in my hands and that any such story was false."

"Didn't he tell you anything further?"

"I believe he asked me who had the best of it and said that if we would pull off and give him a little time he would promise not to shoot any of us when we got out from shelter. I doubted this statement and told him so and he said that whenever he gave his word he kept it. We drew off and as we were leaving he hallooed to me that if I'd fix a bond for him he'd come in and surrender."

"Didn't he tell you that if you would quit opposing his making a bond he would surrender?"

"He seemed to be under the impression that I was opposing it, but I told him that I had nothing to do with his bond."

The note that had been written by Pat Garrett to Oliver Lee after the gun battle inquiring about Kearney's condition was produced.

"Are you positive that either Mr. Lee or Mr. Gililland was lying down on that house [when Garrett returned to get Kearney]?"

"I am positive that Mr. Gililland was. While I was placing Kearney in the wagon and while I was talking to him after the general fight was over two shots were fired from the roof. One of them came down through the wagon shed roof and struck the wheel beside me."

Garrett said he had been at Lee's ranch since the fight looking for Lee.

After a few more questions, the jury was asked to retire, as Fall wanted to ask Garrett certain questions that were ruled inadmissible, but that Fall wanted part of the record nonetheless. After that, midday recess was taken.

Garrett began the afternoon on the stand. The testimony of the famous sheriff brought more women into the courtroom than usual.

Prosecuting attorney Barnes did the re-direct. "Why were bench warrants issued for the defendants?"

"Because their attorneys had access to the grand jury room and had they been indicted I'm satisfied the prisoners would have known it before the officers."

"Did Mr. Kearney make any statement or declaration to you after he was shot?"

"Yes sir, as I was helping him out of the wagon."

Objected to and after an argument, sustained. The next question brought the following answer, "My impression was that Lee's third shot struck Mr. Kearney and that Gililland fired the shot that broke Kearney's leg."

That was also objected to. The question and answer were thrown out.

Barnes asked Garrett, "Did you ever have reason to change your opinion concerning what you said this morning about Ben Williams having a mania for killing?"

"Yes sir," answered Garrett. "I changed it before I employed him as a deputy." Garrett was excused.[7]

Dr. Francis Crosson was called next. Crosson, the Santa Fe chemist to whom Thornton gave the blood samples, was the former assistant chemist at Bellevue Hospital in New York. He had practiced medicine for eleven years and "devoted much study to analyzing blood. . . ." He said that he received a piece of blood-soaked earth and horse hair to analyze on about February 1, 1896.

Crosson testified to the tests he made of the blood, including taking the specific gravity and doing a spectral analysis. He added, "I also tasted it to see whether it was saline or not, which is one of the chemical characteristics of blood."

"Did you make a microscopic examination?"

"I did not at the time." The witness went on to explain the object of the microscopic examination. He used scientific language that stumped the interpreter and caused much laughter in the courtroom. "The conclusion that I reached," stated Crosson, "was that the liquid passed all the characteristics of human blood."

"Was the blood fresh or blood from a sore?" The prosecuting attorney asked.

"It was fresh blood, unmixed with pus. It had soaked into the soil several inches in depth." Crosson said, "a small quantity of blood would not soak very deep in the soil, as blood is composed largely of solid matter and coagulates rapidly. The piece of earth was cone shaped and was dry and glistening at the top where the blood had coagulated. It was chocolate colored."

There was an argument as to the admissibility of Crosson's evidence as to how much blood had been shed. He was temporarily excused and his cross-examination deferred.[8]

John Meadows, a member of one of the initial search parties as well as of the posse that Van Patten led a week or so later, told about the blood spot found where Fountain's buckboard left the road. "The blood spot was surrounded by a sprinkling of blood, which was scattered around the main pool and by actual measurement was found to be eight feet two inches across. The pool in the center was only a few inches in diameter. Van Patten gouged some of the blood and earth up and carried it away."

On cross-examination, Fall established that Meadows had lived in Colorado under the name of John Gray. Fall asked him, "Are you the same John Gray who was indicted in Smith County, Texas, for assault to commit murder and sent to the penitentiary for two years?"

Meadows grew restless, squirmed, and got red in the face. He turned desperately to Judge Parker and pleaded, "If I've got to answer all these questions I claim the right to explain."

Parker told Meadows he could explain and Meadows blurted out, "No, I'm not the same man and never was there! I don't know nothing about that place." The courtroom was instantly filled with an uproar of laughter.

Meadows was then asked to tell how he came by the name of John Gray.

"It just about suits me to tell that. When I was nothin' but a boy I worked for John Selman and John Lawrence [Larn] up about Fort Griffin. I knew them both to be murderers and thieves, but I was nothin' but a boy and I had no sense. People advised me to cut loose from them and I left. The next year people livin' there took old Lawrence out and killed him and Selman was afterwards killed by George Scarborough at El Paso."[9]

"So you are the last of the bunch," remarked Fall, drawing more laughter.

Meadows overlooked the interruption and continued, "Some time ago while fishing with Tom Norris, Billy the Kid, and some other fellows, some men came along and happened to ask what my name was and Norris told them that it was John Gray. That's how I came by that handle. I sailed under it five years."

The spectators, lawyers, defendants, and Judge joined in the laughter created by Meadows's story.[10]

Dr. Crosson was recalled, and after brief questioning, he was passed to Fall. Fall asked some technical questions, such as how long would it take blood to dry in a moist climate, what was specific gravity, and the composition of blood. Then he asked, "What effect would salt in the earth, if there was any, have on your experiment?"

"I don't know. I didn't examine the earth for salt."

"And yet you swear that this blood was human blood?"

"I didn't swear anything of the kind!" Crosson responded. "There is no human being who can tell human blood from any other kind of blood after the red corpuscles have changed construction! But I did swear that my conclusions were that the blood was that of a human being."

"Oh, that's different. That's different. Now, is the specific gravity any conclusive test of blood? Can you tell by that whether blood is that of a horse, a coyote, a rabbit, or a man?"

"I do not know."

Fall questioned Crosson in the same manner regarding the test with litmus paper, and Crosson replied that the test did not provide specific evidence that blood was human blood.

"Will you undertake before this jury to taste samples of human blood, dog's blood, or rat's blood and tell which is human blood?"

"No, I wouldn't."

"That's all."

On redirect the doctor stated, "Blood testing is so difficult that the best expert in the world would not swear to it."[11]

The night session began with Carl Clausen's testimony. Clausen told of trailing the horsemen from Fountain's buckboard. He said he followed a large horse track toward Lee's ranch. The horse had apparently been ridden at night as the trail showed times where the animal had gone straight into mesquite bushes and then turned away.

Clausen told of his experience at Wildy Well. He said, "The first party to come out of the house was a colored man, stepping sideways, in his hand a six-shooter. He stepped slowly until he was past me and then made a dash behind the water tank." Clausen spoke to the second man who came out, but he did not receive an answer. Lee then came out. Lee agreed to let Clausen get water, then asked about the search party. Clausen testified, "I told him we were searching for the Fountains. I asked him why he and his men couldn't go out and assist us. He said he hadn't time and 'what the hell are those sons of bitches to us?' . . . Oliver Lee mounted his horse and taking my back track went straight toward Jarillas. I soon lost sight of him. I examined the trail of his horse and found it to be the same that I had followed." When Clausen entered the house to pay for the water, "three men within hastily sprang up with their hands on their guns and confronted me."

Fall cross-examined the witness. "Did you or did you not, on the road down there to Lee's ranch say to your companion, Luis Herrera, that when Lee came out to give you the wink and you would kill him on the spot? Did you or did you not?"

"I'm sure I did not."

"Did the Negro who came out of the door have a pistol?"

"Yes sir, a big one."

"Isn't it a fact that the Negro had a piece of lead in his hand that he was stopping up leaks in the water tank with and that you mistook the lead for a pistol?"

"It is not a fact, Mr. Fall." Fall then asked Clausen several times if the horse he trailed was shod or not. Each time Clausen answered that it was, to the best of his knowledge.

"Well, was it shod or not?"

At that, Catron objected to Clausen being interrogated in this manner. Fall said he would interrogate the witness to suit himself and advised "the heavy-weight attorney for the prosecution to sit down."

Judge Parker interjected, saying that there had been entirely too much scolding of witnesses and bickering between the attorneys. He ordered them to desist. Barnes conducted the re-direct of Clausen. "Was this the first time that you ever did any trailing, Mr. Clausen?"

"No sir. I trailed in '81, '82, '83, '84, and at other times. In those days Indians were plentiful and a man had to be able to read signs."

"Did you say Mr. Lee saddled the horse he rode away from the ranch?"

"No sir, the horse was already saddled and hitched near the house."[12]

sixteen

The Prosecution Closes

Captain Thomas Branigan led off the next morning's testimony. He said that he knew Lee and McNew but was not well acquainted with Gililland, then described trailing Fountain's buckboard, the Cruces and Tularosa road, and the area around Chalk Hill. He testified to trailing the buckboard to the spot where it was abandoned, and from there to trailing horse tracks that left that spot. He talked about finding an impression on the ground where a blanket had been laid down with something heavy on it.

He went on to describe the remnants of a dry campfire that was five miles from where they had found the buckboard. There were boot tracks surrounding it. Branigan saw the tracks of a child leading away from the fire about six feet. "I do not know how it got there nor where it went, as I could not trail it any further nor back to the fire. My conclusion was that one of the men had taken the child's shoe in his hand or on a stick and made the impressions with it. There were only four tracks and all were made by the shoe belonging to the child's right foot. . . ."

"I measured the tracks of three men about the camp and at other camps along the trail of seven horses from this point, and the next day found tracks on Lee's dirt roof exactly like the one having a heel run over that I found in the camps. When McNew came to Las Cruces a short time later I waited for a chance and measured his tracks. These gave the same measurements as the others about the camp. The track of Lee's horse also corresponded with those of the largest horse on the trail from the camp." Branigan testified that he had measured the tracks carefully from the heel to the toe, across the heel, across the toe, and across the ball of the foot. The measurements to be used as evidence had disappeared from the district attorney's office.

Branigan told of following the trail of the horsemen toward Lee's ranch until a herd of cattle, traveling the direction of the trail, passed by and obliterated it. The men in charge of the herd said they were taking the cattle to Lee's well.

Fall cross-examined the witness.

"How long have you been a scout and trailer?"

"Eighteen years."

"Don't you know that it would be impossible to measure a track in a sandy soil after it had been made?"

"Well, some of them were almost perfect and others were deeper. Sand had fallen in on these and partly obliterated them."

Fall's questioning became tedious as he attempted to show that Branigan was intent on proving that the trail led to Lee's ranch, and that what he wanted was to implicate Lee and no one else. On a few points, Branigan was harassed unmercifully and seemed somewhat confused at times, but stuck to his main narrative.[1]

The next witness was W. T. White. In January 1896, he was helping Dan Fitchett hold a herd of cattle that were to be delivered to Lee's ranch. On the way there, a party came to them and asked whose cattle they were and other questions. He said that when they reached Lee's ranch Gililland, McNew, Blevins, and Lee were there. "McNew went to the house and got his gun as we came up."

"Mr. White," Fall asked during the cross-examination, "in driving cattle from Dog Canyon to Lee's well which is the best route?"

"The one we took."

"As you were going down, which side of you was the posse on when you met it?"

"On the right."

"Then the posse went on around the herd and preceded you to Lee's well?"

"Yes sir."[2]

Irving Wright testified to finding Fountain's mare.

After Wright, the jury was told to retire. The attorneys then proceeded to argue about the admissibility of the testimony of Charles Lusk regarding McNew's statement that Fountain was only prosecuting them to break them apart. Childers argued that circumstantial evidence had demonstrated a conspiracy between the defendants and urged that the evidence of Lusk be allowed.

Fall alleged that the *corpus delecti* must first be absolutely proven and then a conspiracy shown before the evidence was admissible.

Parker, following the long argument, ruled that the declaration McNew made to Lusk was admissible against McNew, and added, "If it is competent to admit evidence that would convict McNew and the defendants it is competent to admit the evidence although McNew is not on trial."[3]

The jury was called back into court, but Lusk was unable to be found. As a result, Humphrey Hill was recalled next and repeated his earlier testimony, followed by Lusk, who also repeated what he had earlier told the court.[4]

Deputy Sheriff Ben Williams was the first man on the stand the next morning. Williams testified to the indictments found against the defendants in Lincoln in 1896. Williams had held warrants for the arrest of the indicted parties. He said that the indictments were found at the insistence of Colonel Fountain.[5]

Charles Lusk was again recalled briefly,[6] followed by William H. H. Llewellyn. The major was ill and his physician was in town. He was likely still suffering from the yellow fever he contracted while serving in the Spanish-American War.[7] Llewellyn said he was a lawyer by profession and in the past had been the district attorney of Doña Ana County, agent on the Mescalero Indian reservation, a member of the State Legislature and speaker of the House of Representatives, and captain of Roosevelt's Rough Riders regiment. Llewellyn said that he knew Colonel Fountain quite well and also his family. He had been in Fountain's home many times and never knew a more affectionate family.

Fall objected here, saying he had no intention of showing anything to Fountain's family relations. Judge Parker asked Catron to point out the materiality of the evidence. Catron stated that Fountain had disappeared and the question had been raised that Fountain might have gone away on account of domestic difficulties. He wanted to prevent anything of the kind. Parker overruled the objection.

The questioning moved on to Llewellyn's actions after Fountain disappeared. Llewellyn said he was requested to form a posse and search for Colonel Fountain. He did so, raising a posse of about twenty-five persons. Llewellyn described the trailing of the buckboard, the remnants of the campfire, the abandoned buckboard, and the tracks around it. "There were three or four child's tracks, all made by the right shoe. The tracks of men were made by cowboy boots; one of the boots was run over at one side. I afterwards saw one pair of these tracks at Wildy's Wells [Wildy Well] and another pair at Las Cruces. I was with Captain Branigan in Las Cruces when William McNew passed along and Captain Branigan measured his tracks and compared them with a pair of the tracks around the camp fire." Llewellyn said he preserved the measurements of the boot and horseshoe tracks, but didn't know what became of them.

Llewellyn testified that they followed the trail of horsemen from the campfire to within six or seven miles of Wildy Well. At that point, a herd of cattle being driven by Dan Fitchett from Dog Canyon to Wildy Well came into the trail.

The questions moved on to Wildy Well. Llewellyn stated that Clausen called his attention to a man on a white horse some distance away. "We examined the tracks and I thought it was the horse that went from the camp fire toward Wildy's Well."

Court adjourned early, 2 o'clock, due to Llewellyn becoming ill. The trial resumed the following day.

When Llewellyn returned to the stand, Albert Fall got his chance at him. Llewellyn denied accusations connecting him with plots to murder Fall, Lee, and others suspected in the case. He admitted to having employed detectives after the case had been given to Garrett. Numerous letters concerning other detectives that were sent between Llewellyn and W. W. Cox were introduced by Fall and identified by Llewellyn. The direct evidence of Llewellyn was not changed materially on cross-examination.[8]

That afternoon, the women of Hillsboro put a large bouquet of flowers in front of the defendants.[9]

Albert Fountain was recalled briefly. He said that he was the first of the search party to find blood and in the excitement thought he saw his father's boot tracks near the blood soaked spot, but was probably mistaken. Some of the men in the posse measured the tracks for future reference. With that, the prosecution closed its case.[10]

The absence of Pinkerton operative John Fraser as a witness must be noted here. Fraser, who was on the prosecution's witness list, was unable to attend the trial because he was returning from Peru with a prisoner. The prisoner was former San Luis Obispo tax collector Samuel Findley, who had embezzled close to $12,000 from the California county and fled to South America, where Fraser found him.[11]

Sierra County Courthouse, circa 1910.
(Date and photographer unknown. Courtesy of New Mexico State
University Library, Archives and Special Collections, Rhea family papers,
Ms00540312.)

Jail cell, Hillsboro, 2004. Left of center is the cell window, which was
cemented over in the early 1900s.
(Author's photograph.)

seventeen

The Defense and Rebuttal

It was now time for the defense to present their case. Their strategy was twofold: attack the credibility of prosecution witnesses and present an alibi for the accused. To open their case, the defense called Tom Tucker to the stand in their first attempt to prove an alibi for the defendants. His testimony was not reported.[1]

Pedro Gonzales, a member of the initial searching party, testified to trailing the buckboard. Gonzales said there were no tracks around the campfire when they arrived. He thought the tracks measured by Llewellyn were tracks of members of the search party. Jacovo Chavez, another search party member, repeated the testimony of Gonzales, also believing that Branigan and Llewellyn measured tracks of search party members.[2]

The next witness called was A. N. Bailey, an employee of Lee, who stated that he was at Lee's Dog Canyon ranch on the day of the disappearance. The defendants were there also.[3] Joe Fitchett testified that he had met Oliver Lee at his Dog Canyon ranch on the day of the disappearance.

Dan Fitchett was called and asked about the cattle he delivered that destroyed the trail that the Llewellyn party followed. As the questioning continued, Fitchett said that he had seen Gililland and McNew at Dog Canyon near sundown on February 1, 1896. He was also at Wildy Well when Clausen was there. He said that Ed, who allegedly had drawn a weapon, was working on a water tank at the time.[4] It's a good guess that in the unreported testimony a claim was made that Ed was holding a piece of lead, and not a gun as Clausen stated.

The defense brought George Curry to the stand. Curry declared that Jack Maxwell had told him that he had slept with McNew at Lee's ranch the night Fountain was killed. Maxwell told him Lee and Gililland were there also. On cross-examination, Curry admitted to owing Lee money.[5]

Bud Smith followed Curry to the stand. Smith, a former employee of Jack Maxwell, stated that Maxwell had told him that he slept with McNew at Lee's ranch the night Fountain was killed. Lee and Gililland were also there.[6] Joe Morgan, the next witness, testified to seeing the defendants at Dog Canyon the day before the disappearance.

The prosecution's cross-examination brought out the friendship and business relations among the witness and the defendants. Morgan admitted to being indicted for murder in Clarksville, Texas, but was never prosecuted for that crime.[7]

The next morning opened with Albert Blevins taking the stand. Blevins, a fireman, said he was working near Lee's ranch on February 1, 1896, and testified that he was with Lee and Gililland the day and night that Fountain and his son disappeared. Blevins arrived there at 2:00 in the afternoon on Saturday, February 1, and remained there until Monday. Jack Maxwell was there also.

Blevins stated that the cattle that the prosecution claimed was used to obliterate the trail were under contract to be delivered, and said Lee was with him the day he met the herd. He refuted the descriptions of the suspicious actions of the defendants in the presence of searchers.

Blevins was questioned for nearly three hours by the prosecution, but nothing was brought out or changed.[8]

Oliver Lee's elderly, widowed mother took the stand next. She testified that her son was at home at the time of Colonel Fountain's disappearance.[9] As Oliver Lee took the stand, women wept and gave him a "soft patting of hands." The courtroom was silent as the defendant testified.

Lee said he did not learn that he was a suspect until several days after the disappearance. Upon hearing that he was suspected, he went to Las Cruces, found the warrant issued, and went to the authorities to surrender, but was refused.[10] He learned of a posse searching for him and that among the members was Ben Williams, who was said to have a mania for murder, and others who were known to be enemies.[11]

Lee stated that an extra issue of a Las Cruces paper advocated mob law and openly accused him of the Fountain murder. Fall intended to introduce the newspaper as evidence but the prosecution objected. Fall argued that he could point to, in the courtroom, the man who wrote the article. Parker ruled that the newspaper could not be introduced as evidence, but permitted Lee to testify as to how he had been affected by the publication of articles.

Lee described how he had heard that officers intended to kill him "with warrants for the murder of Fountain as an excuse." As a result, Lee hurried home to his ranch. He returned to Las Cruces several times and learned that the warrants had been withdrawn. The matter, he said, was especially rife at election time. Lee testified that he did not surrender when the last warrant was issued because of mob talk and of information that certain men had said that they would "deal him violence" if he came in.

Fall then asked Lee about the killing of Kent Kearney at Wildy Well. Lee stated that he slept on the roof because he was afraid that Pat Garrett and his crowd would kill him while he slept.

"I was asleep when fired upon," Lee testified. "Kearney fired twice and Garrett also fired before I fired. I heard no commands of 'hands up,' but Garrett was talking while shooting. We killed Kearney. We took care of him and made him as comfortable as possible while dying. We made the Garrett party ride away, but agreed to surrender on condition that Garrett would tell the truth about the matter. I was waiting for a new sheriff to be put in Doña Ana County before surrendering. We were at Dog Canyon almost every day soon after Fountain's disappearance and neither Pat Garrett nor any other officer came after us at that place."

On cross-examination, Childers asked Lee who told him that Garrett had threatened him. Fall objected and asked to be allowed to make a statement. The jury was then excused. Fall told the court that if Lee answered the question, it would place a life in jeopardy. Fall told Parker that Garrett had said he would whip any man stating on the witness stand that he had threatened Lee. Parker allowed the question and the jury was recalled.

Lee said that Albert Ellis told him that Garrett had said no one need fear Lee if he was given a warrant for Lee's arrest.

Court was adjourned for the night and the questioning of Lee was picked up the next morning.[12]

Childers asked Lee if he knew anything about what Fall did to secure the appointment of Pat Garrett as sheriff. Lee said he had heard a good deal of talk about it, and he had some conversation with Fall about it, but he could not recall the exact words.

"Didn't Fall try to get Garrett appointed sheriff so as to keep Numa Reymond out of the place?"

"I know nothing about that."

Childers asked several more questions along the same line.

Childers then asked, "Did you know Charles Rodius and Mark Coffelt?"

"Yes."

"Did you have anything to do with killing them?"

The defense of course objected to this line of questioning. Fall admitted that Lee had killed Rodius, but objected to the introduction of evidence based on only indictments. Fall argued that evidence not relating to the case at issue could not be considered competent unless a conviction was shown in order to impeach the character or credibility of the witness. The jury was dismissed and, after considerable argument, the evidence was ruled inadmissible.

The cross-examination ended there. On re-direct, Lee stated that he had been involved in several business ventures with Fall since 1889, besides the personal relationship that existed.

Fall asked, "You stated in cross-examination that you thought Llewellyn, Lohman, and Numa Reymond were against you. Have you any reason to think that Reymond is an enemy of yours? If so, why?"

"One of the strongest things that make me think he is an enemy is a couple of letters written by Bob Burch and Jeff Aiks, stating that they had been approached and offered money to kill myself and Fall."

The prosecution objected on the grounds that the letters were not in evidence. The court sustained the objection unless the letters themselves could be accounted for in some way. Lee was asked and said he did not know where the letters were. Fall was sworn in and testified that he looked for the letters recently, but could not find them. He said he had seen the letters since they were received and had read them to the parties themselves. They were dated in June and July 1896.

Fall then questioned Lee again. "Did the letters state as to who would pay the money?"

Lee answered that his understanding was that Numa Reymond had offered to put up the money.

"Have you heard any talk as to Reymond putting up money against you?"

Prosecution objected. Sustained.

"Besides the witness Maxwell, have you heard of any other witnesses having been offered money to testify falsely?"

Objected to and sustained.

It came out next that W. W. Cox, a former friend of William Llewellyn who was now friendly with Oliver Lee, had said that Jake

Ryan was paid to kill both Lee and Fall. Cox said he had found Ryan lying in wait. The money, care of Llewellyn, was to be paid Ryan via the New York Exchange.

Childers followed the defense with a few more questions for Lee. He asked Lee how he became a deputy sheriff.

"Oh," said Lee, "there was a good deal of talk around Las Cruces about Ben Williams, that he was bulldozing the Sheriff and making trouble generally. The citizens were very indignant, and when I went there, I had no more sense than to let them appoint me deputy sheriff. I soon after disarmed Williams."

"You were appointed especially to take in Williams?"

"I believe there was some talk about it. I wouldn't tell him that."

In reply to another question, Lee said that Burch and Aiks were offered five thousand dollars to kill himself and Fall.

Childers asked Lee who had informed him that Reymond was going to put up the money against him.

Lee protested to bringing in the names of a lot of citizens, and asked Childers to refrain from questioning him in detail on that matter, saying that of course if questioned he would have to answer, being under oath. Lee said, "It had been stated that Reymond was to pay." Childers did not press the question. Lee was dismissed.[13]

James Wharton was called to the stand. Wharton stated that he was a resident of White Oaks, Lincoln County, and was the district attorney there in January 1896. He was asked what connection Colonel Fountain had had with the indictments that were found against the defendants during that term of court.

The witness testified that so far as he knew, Fountain had nothing to do with procuring the indictments or trying the cattle cases that were before the court, contradicting the testimony of Theodore Herman, the foreman of the jury in Lincoln. Wharton stated that Fountain was not before the grand jury at that term. Les Dow was working up the cases, and witness consulted with Dow and others, but not with Fountain. Fountain had no court papers, that is no official documents, relating to the cattle cases in his possession when he left Lincoln. He said that the indictments against the defendants were dismissed when the case came to trial.

"Did the prosecution of these cases depend in any manner upon Colonel Fountain?" Fall asked Wharton.

Objected to and overruled.

"It did not."

Then came the cross-examination. "What about the killing of Les Dow? Was it before or after the next succeeding term of court?"

"It was before the term at which the indictments were dismissed. I think it was before the next term."

Objected to and overruled.[14]

John H. May took the stand but said nothing of value.[15]

Philip S. Fall, the brother of defense attorney Albert Fall, took the stand to begin the afternoon session. Philip Fall stated that he currently lived in Mexico, but in 1896 he was a resident of Las Cruces where he was a deputy sheriff. He said that about the third of February he told Lee that there were warrants out for Gilliland, Jack Tucker, and McNew. He went with Lee and Tom Tucker to the office of the justice of the peace and asked who had the warrants, but Justice of the Peace Valdez said he was too sick to tell. They then went to District Attorney Young's office. Young said he did not know who had the warrants nor did he know anything of the circumstances of the complaint. After seeing Guadalupe Ascarate and Joe Morgan, it was agreed that a posse would go out after McNew, Gilliland, and Jack Tucker. Philip Fall, Morgan, Tom Tucker, Howard Ellis, and Lee went together and found McNew and Gilliland at Dog Canyon. They all went from there to Wildy Well, where they found three deputies who had a note from Young saying that the cases had been dismissed and there was no need to come in.[16]

The next witness called for the defense was Print Rhodes. Rhodes testified that he lived about ten miles from Cox's ranch and was a brother-in-law to Lee. He knew Llewellyn and José Espalin. He said that in the evening of about July 11, 1898, he saw Lee and Espalin at Cox's ranch. While there, Lee and Gililland rode up to the gate and Espalin went out and shook hands with them. They left and had been gone about ten or fifteen minutes when Espalin asked Rhodes to go with him to speak with Lee. Rhodes said after they had gone a short distance, Espalin stopped and said, "Maybe I'd better not go." Espalin said he knew men were going to kill Lee, and he asked Rhodes tell him to look out. Rhodes caught up with Lee and told him Espalin's message.

Rhodes testified to a talk he had had with William Llewellyn shortly after Fountain disappeared. Fall asked Rhodes if Llewellyn told him, "there was nothing he would not stoop to, to connect Lee with this case?"

Rhodes said he did. Under cross-examination by Childers, Rhodes said he talked with Llewellyn at his camp "in the flats" about a week or two after Fountain disappeared. Llewellyn said he had been over the mountain to see if Oliver Lee was in town. There were five or six fellows with him and they had put their horses inside an adobe wall alongside the road and had hidden themselves. They sent a man into town who was to watch Lee and when Lee started out the runner would come out ahead of him and notify the men in hiding. "They were to lay there in them walls and kill Lee when he came out," Rhodes testified. Llewellyn told him that he had been there a part of the day when the runner came out he told them that Lee had gone out the other way.

Rhodes testified, "Llewellyn said he wouldn't stop at anything to do those fellers. He said his [wagon] was a settin' there with dynamite in it. If there was any woman in there [Lee's house] he would invite 'em out. If they didn't come out he would throw the dynamite in and blow 'em up."

Rhodes claimed that while he was at camp, a man named Fowler told Llewellyn, loud enough for everyone to hear, "If you are going to do this job you better get to it. If not, I am going back to town." Rhodes then went back to his house. Rhodes said later on Llewellyn and the others came to his house and he gave them coffee. Llewellyn came inside. Rhodes testified that in the presence of his wife Llewellyn repeated his threat to blow Lee up with dynamite. The spectators, mostly pro-defense, nearly burst forth in cheers at the revelation.[17]

Childers asked, "Did Llewellyn seem to have his senses that day, the day he did all that talking?"

"About as much senses as he ever had, I guess." Rhodes's reply caused much laughter.

Rhodes brought a good deal of hilarity to the courtroom with the jury, attorneys, and spectators laughing through much of his testimony. When Childers asked on what night he saw Lee and Espalin at Cox's ranch, Rhodes responded, "The night before the rumpus." Childers's effort to elicit a definition of the word "rumpus" caused a great deal of amusement in the courtroom.

The defense rested. Recess was taken until about 7:30 p.m. to give the prosecution time to prepare their rebuttal.[18]

That evening, the prosecution called David Sutherland to the stand to begin their rebuttal. Sutherland swore that Dan Fitchett told him he went to Lee's ranch on the morning, not the evening, of February 1, 1896, and found Lee there setting out grapevines. Fitchett told Sutherland that he "didn't believe those boys were guilty for he saw them in the morning of that day at Lee's ranch."[19]

Next, Pat Garrett testified to a conversation with Fitchett that corroborated Sutherland's testimony.[20] Thomas Branigan took the stand to rebut the evidence of Print Rhodes in regards to Llewellyn. Branigan testified that during the first half of February 1896, he was camped in "the flats," about two miles from Rhodes's house.

With Branigan was Carl Clausen, William Llewellyn, Jack Fountain, Tom Fountain, Ben Williams, and Fowler. Branigan said that he did not see Rhodes at the camp and said he would likely have seen him had he come in at any time. Branigan was at the camp most of the time. He did not hear Fowler remark, "If you are going to do this job you had better get to it, or I am going back to town," as was attributed to him by Rhodes. The party, which Branigan was a member of, never put their horses in an adobe enclosure or lay in wait to kill Lee. Branigan smiled at the absurdity of the question. He said the party stopped at Rhodes's house on the way to Las Cruces and that he was with Llewellyn all the time he was there. He claimed that Llewellyn did not enter the house at any time, nor did he have any conversation with Rhodes at that time. Branigan was very positive that none of the conversation detailed by Rhodes could have taken place without his knowing it.[21]

Carl Clausen followed Branigan with much the same testimony. Clausen was more positive than Branigan that Rhodes was not at the camp at any time and that Llewellyn had not talked to Rhodes at his house. Only Williams went inside the house, he said. Clausen and Llewellyn were side by side the entire time that they were there.

On cross-examination, Fall asked, "Did not Llewellyn send Luis Herrera into Las Cruces with a note to Oscar Lohman asking where Lee was, and did he not get an answer saying Lee had gone out another way?" Fall said Herrera was the courier referred to by Rhodes.

Clausen answered, "No."

"Did Tom Fountain leave the camp at any time you were there?"

"I don't think so; he may have."

Fall remarked that while the witness testified very positively that Rhodes did not come to the camp at any time, he was uncertain as to whether Tom Fountain went out or not.

Clausen admitted to not having been at the camp the entire time.[22]

Jack Fountain's testimony corroborated that of the previous two witnesses.[23]

José Espalin took the stand. He testified that on July 11, 1898, he was at Cox's ranch and saw Lee, Gililland, and Rhodes. Lee and Gililland stopped a few minutes and when they left, they went toward the Jarillas. Espalin said that he never said to Rhodes that he would like Rhodes to go with him as he wanted to speak with Lee and he did not tell Rhodes that anybody was going to kill Lee or say anything like it.

Fall questioned the witness. "Did you have a talk about three weeks ago with Don Pinito Pino and José Armijo about Lee and Gililland and the Fountain case?"

"I may have."

"Did you not say that you intended to go on the stand and help Lee and these boys but after the fight at Parker's Well Tom Tucker had called you a [God damn?] sneak and a coward and now you would go on the stand and swear against them?"

"No, I was told Tucker had called me a coward, but I said I believed that Tucker was straight and that he did not say it."

Objected to by the prosecution and sustained.

Fall asked, "How much money did you get off that Negro you murdered at Fort Selden three years ago?"

Objected to and sustained, obviously.

In answering further questions, Espalin said he was a deputy sheriff in July 1898. He went back and reported to Garrett after he had seen Lee. He denied having said "*Cuidado* [be careful]" as a warning to Lee as he said goodbye.[24]

The prosecution then brought three successive witnesses to refute a statement Tom Tucker had made about the hind feet of Lee's white horse being larger than the fore feet. After much time had been consumed, Fall admitted that Tucker had misspoke.[25]

Jack Maxwell was brought back to the stand to rebut the testimony of Bud Smith, who claimed that Maxwell said, "It would be useless to try to connect Lee with the Fountain case . . . ." On cross-examination, he admitted that he had had some such conversation.[26]

The prosecution called one more witness. It was a fitting end considering the problems the prosecution had had with witnesses throughout the trial. The *El Paso Herald* reported, "A man named Wright was brought on to testify, it is to be presumed, to something. Mr. Childers made repeated attempts to get that something out of the witness but the witness seemed to be in a sort of stupor and wasn't exactly satisfactory."

At last, Childers asked, "Well, do you know anything about it at all?"

"No sir," said the witness.

"That's all."[27]

eighteen

Closing Arguments and the Verdict

Before the closing arguments began, the attorneys argued as to whether the defendants could be found guilty of murder in the first, second, or third degree, or if it was to be first degree or nothing at all. The defense wanted only the latter option available to the jury. Judge Parker ruled, "The court will submit the three degrees of murder to the jury."[1]

The jury was brought in. Richmond Barnes opened the closing arguments for the prosecution. Barnes went through the chain of circumstantial evidence very thoroughly. He said that while one or a few coincidences might be explained, the whole chain could only be explained on the one hypothesis, that the defendants had murdered the Fountain child. His speech was described as "rather flowery, and the figures of speech and quotations from *The Pickwick Papers* probably went over the heads of the jury." The interpreter had a difficult time translating some of this, and Barnes had to repeat his expressions. When speaking of Oliver Lee's mother, who had testified as to Lee's alibi, Barnes remarked that she had laid "a wreath of maternal duty on the altar of maternal love." This was too much for the interpreter, and the prosecutor had to explain. Barnes spoke until the noon recess.[2]

That afternoon, Harvey Fergusson began the argument for the defense. He took up the witnesses for the prosecution one after the other and attempted to discredit them. He talked straight to the jury and once called a juror by name. He spent much time questioning the credibility of Jack Maxwell.

Fergusson said that he would consider the evidence introduced by the prosecution just as if no evidence at all had been introduced by the defense. He stated that he would show the weakness of the case against the defendants. "You are trying these men for the killing of a little boy, but you cannot connect the blood spot with the Fountain boy. There is not any proof that it was human blood."

He spoke of Dr. Crosson, "who said that no expert could be sure the blood was not that of a horse, a coyote, a dog, or a beef . . . . To convict in this case you have got to be sure that that blood was the blood of the boy Fountain."

He said that Albert J. Fountain, the soul of honor, would not lend himself to the work of Llewellyn and Branigan, and testified that to the best of his knowledge and belief the tracks of a boy around the campfire were those of his little brother and were naturally made.

"You must be certain not only that circumstances show that these defendants committed a crime at the place and time charged in the indictment, but that a crime was committed. Does any of the evidence submitted show that beyond a reasonable doubt?"

Fergusson questioned whether the blood spot, which wasn't found on the initial search, could have gotten there some other way. "Albert Fountain examined the tracks of the buggy and the horses with minute care, so that he was able to swear that they were thus and so in great detail, but he swore that he saw no blood spot. . . . Why was there no blood on the buckboard, not a sign? Who drove the buckboard after the three men had surrounded the vehicle and Fountain had been killed? Did the boy drive? Then was he dead? Was the boy alive at the campfire, where his tracks were found? Might he not have been abducted? The mail driver testified that the blood was partly fresh nine days after the disappearance. Did he not see it soon after it had been spilled there? Was it there at all the day after the disappearance? There was nothing to show that it was."

Fergusson discredited the measurements of tracks and said it would be impossible to identify a man by his boot tracks in the sand. There was nothing to show that the three horse tracks had even been made at the same time as the buggy tracks, he said. Who would swear that they were not made an hour before or an hour after? He argued that it had taken very little to confirm to the search party their suspicions.

Court took a recess and resumed that evening with Fergusson picking up his address. He posed the question, what was there against Gililland? He said only Riley Baker and the Goulds, who were "personal enemies of Gililland," testified against him, and they only testified to an "alleged remark" that may not have even referred to Fountain. He stated,

> The prosecution had to get three such men to testify against Gililland because that trivial incident was all they could find against him. They had to have three men because there were three tracks to fill, and since Lee and McNew did not fill the bill, they picked out Gililland. It was true that those men were all indicted at that term of court, but there were fifteen or twenty indicted at the same time. Why did they pick out Gililland? Even if it had been shown that Colonel Fountain had never prosecuted anyone else than the defendants, that would not have been sufficient motive for this heinous crime. As a matter of fact, this alleged 'motive' applies to too many men in the territory, as we all know. There must be a grave doubt in your minds, as to the guilt of those defendants. The jury has got to be certain beyond a reasonable doubt that these two men killed little

Henry Fountain at the time and place specified in
the indictment. Can you say that?

Fergusson went on to discuss the "political and personal ani-
mus" in the case:

> I was staggered by the showing made here of the
> state of affairs in Doña Ana County. Is it any wonder
> that Lee was afraid to surrender to a posse under
> Garrett of which Ben Williams was a member? . . .
> The defendants resisted arrest simply so as to make
> sure that they would not have to surrender to their
> personal enemies, possibly at the imminent risk of
> their lives, in order to get a fair trial. They finally
> made arrangements with the Governor of the ter-
> ritory that they should be protected from violence,
> and that "mad dog" should be muzzled and kept
> out of the way. In Doña Ana County, there was a
> fearful state of affairs. The newspapers there were
> practically advocating mob violence against these
> defendants. In view of all the evidence the jury must
> decide whether the existing state of affairs warranted
> Lee and Gililland in wanting to keep out of the way
> of that mob.

"Sheriff Garrett by his evidence that Kearney fired the first shot
in that fight of July 1898 lifts all burden from Lee for the killing of
Kearney. . . . Sheriff Garrett has proved himself to be an honorable
man, but he did not appoint honorable men as his deputies. Why
was it necessary for him to appoint Ben Williams, that 'maniac on
the subject of killing,' and other thoroughly bad men, like this fellow
Espalin, on his posse, when there were so many good citizens of Doña
Ana County who would have been willing to serve on the posse?"

Fergusson said Fall was one of the men these people were after and they believed that, "the verdict would set Fall right . . . ."

"Now I am willing to give my clients' case into your hands. Before you find the defendants guilty you must be certain beyond a reasonable doubt that they killed Henry Fountain. No fair-minded man could so see it. I am certain there can be no conviction."[3]

When court convened the next morning, attendance was about half that of the previous day. William Childers addressed the jury for the prosecution.

Childers talked about the effort the defense had gone to in an attempt to discredit Dr. Crosson and his testimony concerning the blood. "He said that the blood had every characteristic of human blood and that he believed it was human blood. Nobody has shown on this stand that any other animal had been killed there subsequent to the Fountain disappearance. All the other circumstances are such as to make it certain that this was human blood. . . .

"Mr. Fergusson has told you that it would be impossible to measure or identify horse or man tracks, especially if the wind was blowing, and that there is absolutely nothing in such evidence. You well know that the trailing of horses and men is an everyday occurrence in this county, and that to men familiar with the tracking of individuals or parties by such means the work is easy and certain. It is utter nonsense to talk about obliteration of such tracks in a week or even two weeks. If they are lost for a time that can be picked up farther on."

Childers attacked the defense claim that there was not enough of a motive to commit the crime, he said, "There has been ample evidence introduced here to show that these defendants were in fact afraid of Colonel Fountain, and that they were glad he was out of the way after his death." He continued:

> These men had no reason to resist arrest. They
> need not have been afraid of the Sheriff. Garrett

is an honorable man. The defense has paid him a great tribute for his honor and truth. They would have been safe in his hands. They need not have surrendered to that man Williams, if they were indeed afraid of him, which appears ridiculous. No, they were afraid of a newspaper, that little four by nine sheet. Why should they be afraid on account of the utterances of an idiotic newspaperman? Was there not all the law and power of the territory on the side of order and safety? Lee went in and out of Las Cruces without fear up to March 1898. He was not afraid. McNew was in the custody of Sheriff Garrett for many months. He was not killed, or mobbed, or threatened. . . . The defense lay much stress on the claim that it was only after the Governor, by permission of the court, had agreed to protect them from violence and permitted them to surrender outside of Doña Ana County, that the defendants felt willing to surrender themselves for trial. On the contrary, the Governor arranged with these fugitives from justice to surrender in another county simply in order to take away their last excuse for resisting arrest.

Childers stated that Jack Maxwell's reward was not unusual. "When the Governor offers a reward for a fugitive, it is the same thing." He then took up the matter of the alibi. He considered the evidence of each witness in detail. He said because Garrett's testimony on the Kearney fight was so highly praised by the defense, he must have been telling the truth when he said Dan Fitchett told him he went to the Lee ranch in the morning, not the evening, and saw the defendant and others engaged in setting out grapevines.

"Jack Maxwell and the witnesses for the defense agree on every point as to the circumstances and happenings at the ranch Saturday,

Sunday, and perhaps Monday, except that Maxwell says the defendants and McNew were not there Saturday night. Maxwell must be telling the truth, for the witnesses for the defense had every reason to misrepresent the true state of affairs. Maxwell was disinterested." he said the Goulds and Baker

> were also worthy of belief. To hold that you cannot convict of murder because the body cannot be found is to condone murder, to put a premium on crime. You cannot so hold. It is so easy in this country to waylay a man and conceal his body where it cannot be found. There is every evidence that these three men were the perpetrators of this crime. These men have wholly failed to explain any of the incriminating circumstances that form the web we have woven so tightly around them, but instead of refuting our evidence, they have resorted to mud-slinging and have raised the cry of politics.

He concluded: "Gentlemen, leave out every consideration or issue but the one you are called upon to decide. Did these defendants murder that boy? That is what you have got to determine."[4]

That afternoon Harry Daugherty addressed the jury for the defense. Daugherty began by stating that it was not their responsibility to determine the facts in the case, just to show that the defendants had nothing to do with it.

"There has been much confusion in this case. These defendants are not on trial for the killing of Colonel Fountain or Deputy Kearney. They are on trial for killing a little child. Fix that fact firmly in your minds. The imagination of some of the witnesses for the prosecution is of the dime novel order. They can, it seems, tell all about the feeling and thoughts of people from their tracks."

He attacked the prosecuting attorneys. "The prosecution brought politics and outside issues into this case to prejudice the minds of the jury. They try to make these men out to be murderers, desperados, and fugitives from justice. The defense has had to go to a certain extent into the facts about the real conditions at Las Cruces in order to show that it was not for the murder of Henry Fountain, but for personal and political reasons, that these defendants were prosecuted."

Daugherty addressed the missing Fountain bodies. "You have heard much about the *corpus delicti*. Understand me, it is not necessary in order to convict for murder that the body of the victim be produced. But it is customary to bring into court some part of the body, or something that carries absolute conviction that a crime has been committed." He said he had never heard of a case going before a jury without any proof that a crime had even been committed.

Daugherty continued, "Mr. Childers laid stress upon the fact that we had not shown that the blood was not Colonel Fountain's, hence it must be Fountain's. We do not have to show any such thing. . . . They must show that it does come from Colonel Fountain, if they want to prove him dead. Have they shown any such thing?"

Daugherty questioned the motive. "Whatever you may think as to a possible motive for killing Colonel Fountain, there could have been no motive for killing that little boy. It is silly to assume that Lee and Gililland would think that by killing this man and his little boy they could escape all further prosecution, if they were indeed guilty of anything. Did all justice and law in the territory of New Mexico depend, then, on Colonel Fountain? It is absurd."

Daugherty said that the prints of a boy's feet around the campfire were of both feet. "If the alleged murderers tried to deceive with the shoe of the boy why did they not do the same with Fountain's shoes? It is a silly story."

He continued his attack on the search party's testimony. "After the agents of the prosecution had measured the tracks so carefully would they not then have simply the measurements of a certain size of cowboy boot? How many men wear a number seven, or a number six, or number eight boot in this territory? And yet, the only thing they want conviction on is the tracks comparison and measurement. No man saw these defendants on the road. No one saw them kill Colonel Fountain. No one saw them bear the body away. No one knows that Colonel Fountain is dead." Daugherty attacked the prosecution for the missing measurements and challenged the prosecution to produce them. "They say, when asked to produce them, 'We have them not.' A wonderful chain of disappearances in this case, to be sure."

"Everything goes to show that the prosecution in this case had a preconceived opinion that these men did the deed, and they did all they could to fasten it on them. They did not show proper judgment or common sense. They made no effort to find out the real criminals. . . .

"Did Oliver Lee have any motive for resisting arrest? Read the *Doña Ana Republican* four days after the disappearance. It says, 'If Colonel Fountain is dead there can be no question as to whose door the blame lies,' thus in effect charging Oliver Lee with the crime. The posse did not want to arrest Lee and bring him in, but they wanted to carry his dead body to Las Cruces; that is what they wanted, and Lee knew that he would have to protect himself from violence."

He said he believed defense witnesses were telling the truth. "By innuendo they charged Mrs. Lee, the old mother of Oliver Lee, with perjury. They did it in pretty words, but the district attorney had to do it in order to open his attack, and then he put up against that lovely old lady, on the verge of the grave, testifying to the truth under her solemn oath. He put up against her a man who had jumped from place to place all his life and had changed his name with every jump . . . . The man with the two thousand dollar contract is then the only one out of six men and one woman that told the truth. Does that look reasonable? . . . Suppose Colonel

Fountain and that boy should walk into this courtroom tomorrow. Where could you put your finger on a single iota of evidence that would be worth a thought?"[5]

Albert Fall rose to speak next. Fall initially had asked Fergusson and Daugherty to make the closing arguments. Fall was burnt and weak from the long trial, but when Lee found out Fall wasn't planning on speaking to the jury, he requested that Fall reconsider.

Fall responded, "Both Mr. Fergusson and Mr. Daugherty are more eloquent than I. My exhaustion is so great that I doubt my ability to even stand on my feet for ten minutes. I'm afraid I would weaken the case by speaking in my diminished condition."

"Fall," Lee pleaded, "they are trying to hang me for something I am not guilty of."

"All of the evidence is in and they know you are not guilty," Fall replied.

"You know what I would do for you if you were in trouble."[6]

So Fall stepped before the jury. He placed his hands on the rail. He began by talking of the jury system and its great benefits. Fall spoke in a low voice that gradually increased in both volume and pitch as he went on.

Fall questioned the importance of Colonel Fountain in the indictments from the term of court in Lincoln. He said that if the indictments were the motive for murder, why did they not also murder Les Dow and the district attorney?

"As to the alibi, if you believe that that man Maxwell told the truth, you must believe that Blevins—is a liar; that Joe Fitchett—is a liar; that Dan Fitchett—is a liar; that Bailey—is a liar; that Oliver Lee—is a liar; that Mrs. Lee—is a liar. . . . If you believe that Maxwell told the truth, you must believe that George Curry is a liar; and that Bud Smith is a liar. Now take your choice: either all these eight witnesses are liars, or Jack Maxwell is a liar. . . .

"The territory has not done its duty. It has not been hunting for the real murderers of Colonel Fountain and his little boy. It has exerted all its power, and has spent its money, to fasten the crime on these men. . . . I ask for no white mantle of charity for these men. I desire no vindication. I ask simply stern justice. If the evidence in this case convinces you that these men murdered little Henry Fountain, you must convict. There is no alternative. If you are not so convinced, turn them loose." Waxing poetic, Fall thundered:

> You are no doubt surprised to learn that such a state of affairs can exist as that in Doña Ana County. In many streams there is a point at a sharp bend in the course where the water pauses in its onward flow and forms an eddy. Around the edges the slime gathers, and the froth, and logs, and dead leaves, and all manner of floating filth. The moss and ferns grown dank, and the shadowy places are haunted with creeping things. Snakes come out of their hiding places and bask in the sun on the slimy logs, and if they are disturbed in their retreat they sting in the heel the man who is so foolish as to venture there. Doña Ana County is just such a dead eddy. Under the territorial form of government, the public officers do not hold office by the choices of the sovereign people, but are appointed by the federal powers. There in Doña Ana there have gathered together, as does the slimy filth on the edges of the dead eddy, a lot of broken down old political hacks. They bask in the sun of political preferment, like the serpents stretched out on the dead logs. They never got an honest dollar in their lives, and do not know how to earn one except by serving the people, forsooth, in public office. It was in just such a dead eddy as I have described that there arose this plot for the persecution of Oliver Lee.

> Gentlemen of the jury, the prosecution of Oliver
> Lee is the result of a conspiracy to send an innocent
> man to the gallows.

One can just imagine Fall pointing out each person as he said, "The District Attorney is involved in that conspiracy. The honorable Thomas B. Catron is involved in that conspiracy. His honor at the bench is involved in that conspiracy."

At that, Judge Parker jumped up, pounded his gavel, and angrily said, "Mr. Fall, unless you withdraw your remarks about this court from the jury immediately, I shall send you to jail for contempt."

Fall arrogantly replied, "Your honor will not send me to jail for contempt until I am through addressing this jury. When I finish my argument, you may do whatever you wish."

Parker did not press the issue. He knew that any attempt to stop Fall from speaking would be construed, by the many armed Lee-Gililland supporters in the courtroom, as an attempt to prevent Lee and Gililland from receiving a fair trial.

Fall continued. He spoke about how charges were not brought against the defendants for two years, and what an absurd thought it was that he had so much control of the courts. No, he said, they just wanted tools of their own in before charges were brought.

"Our defense is an alibi clearly proved." Fall finished by saying that they had been trying for three years to get this case before a jury. "At last we have our opportunity, and confident that you will do your duty, the highest appertaining to American citizenship, as befits men, we leave the lives of these two men in your hands."

The courtroom filled with applause. When Parker was finally able to quiet the courtroom, a recess was taken. Court resumed at 8:00 that evening.[7]

Thomas Catron closed the case that night in Hillsboro, in front of a packed house. Catron began, "We have endeavored on behalf of the prosecution to present before you evidence to satisfy you as to the true state of facts." He dismissed the politics brought into the case as an attempt by the defense to

> complicate this case with matters that are entirely irrelevant. They have striven by every means in their power to prejudice you, gentlemen of the jury, against not only the witnesses for the prosecution, but against the counsel on this side as well.
>
> I care nothing about the slurs and insinuations that may be thrown out against myself. I have been in this country too long and I am too old a man to take notice of such things. . . . But I do not like to have matters brought up before a jury in order to influence them, that are not connected with the case on trial in any possible way.

Catron moved on to linking the events and evidence together chronologically. He began before the murder took place, with the testimony of Frank Wayne. Wayne had said that Lee remarked, "You boys say nothing about what you saw here, as it might interfere with some of our plans."

What were these plans? Catron described the indictments obtained in Lincoln as a motive. He said that a week before February 1, Gililland came to McNew's house for a fresh horse and cartridges.

> He said, "If anybody inquires for me while I am away, tell them I have gone to Roswell." But he did not go to Roswell. He went to Lee's Dog Canyon ranch. What connection was this with Lee's "plans"?
>
> Tom Tucker was there too, the man who bears the earmarks of the notorious Tewksbury feud. He was a deputy sheriff at Santa Fe, three hundred miles

away. What was he doing there? He had come down and then telegraphed back for his gun and saddle. Had this any connection with Oliver Lee's "plans"?

The defense say they have proved an alibi; that there is nothing but Maxwell's evidence against six other witnesses. If that were true, we would say there would be certainly a reasonable doubt as to the guilt of these men. But when a reputable witness is corroborated by all the accompanying circumstances, those circumstances stand over, against all the verbal evidence that may be brought against him. In this case, everything corroborates the statement of Maxwell that the three men were away from Lee's ranch on the night of February 1st. We have ample evidence to show that the three men left Dog Canyon ranch in plenty of time to reach Luna's Wells. Did they get there? This will determine Maxwell's truth.

The three men assembled in La Luz the night Fountain slept there, Catron said. "Blevins was brought from Texas to fix up the alibi of the defendants and make their trail complete. This being true there are good grounds for suspecting that all the alibi is fixed up. Joe Fitchett looked no man in the face when he testified. Mrs. Lee said that Joe Fitchett had told her that he was going back to his brother's house when he left the ranch. He didn't go. Why all this concealment? Dan Fitchett told Pat Garrett and David Sutherland that he went to the ranch Saturday morning and found the defendants there. There is evidence that he misstated the facts when he said on the witness stand that he went there in the evening. . . . They fixed it so each man would say the others were there. When men of Oliver Lee's intelligence commit a crime, they take care to fix up all details."

186 — Murder on the White Sands

Catron moved on to Chalk Hill, the tracks, the imprints from someone kneeling behind a bush. "Do you believe that the blood is the blood of anybody else than Colonel Fountain? His buggy was left there on the plain, his horses turned loose. Part of his clothing and part of that of the boy was left there. They say he might have got out of the country. How? Did he fly? Had he wings? No, that is impossible. If Colonel Fountain and that little boy had gone out of the country, they would certainly have left some track, some mark, some memory, something to show whither they went. . . . No, he did not get away, except as he and his little boy were carried away, corpses."

He continued, "They say there could have been no motive for the killing of the little boy, even admitting that there was one for the murder of his father. No motive? Suppose the boy was alive at the campfire, did not that little fellow know who killed his father? The murderers had to do away with the boy. He would have identified them without doubt. They could not conceal him with any safety to themselves. They had to kill. They were determined to finish their work."

The defendants, Catron said, behaved suspiciously after the disappearance. He talked about how Lee and Gililland continually avoided arrest and said that the conspiracy to kill Lee and Fall was pure nonsense.

"If these circumstances do not point to these men as the murderers, where else do they point? Explain them if you can."

Catron finished at 10:30 that night. A five-minute recess was taken.[8]

Court resumed five minutes later. The room was quiet as Parker read the charges and instructions to the jury. When Parker finished, he sent the jury to their sleeping quarters. Fall stepped up and insisted they be brought back; the defense demanded a verdict. Parker, as he had done many times already, acceded to Fall's wishes. The jury was brought back and sent to the jury room to deliberate.

It took less than eight minutes to reach a verdict. It was one minute before midnight when the jury foreman handed the verdict to the clerk. The clerk read the few words handed him, ending with, "We find the defendants, Oliver Lee and James Gililland, not guilty."

The verdict was received with applause as Lee, Gililland, and McNew, who sat by the defendants, were immediately swamped by the crowd of well-wishers. The congratulations continued for half an hour.[9]

As the defendants, defense attorneys, and crowd of defense supporters celebrated into the night, the bodies of Albert J. Fountain and his young son Henry lay buried somewhere in the vast New Mexico desert.

Following the trial, Lee and Gililland remained in the custody of Sheriff Curry and were held in the new jail in Alamogordo since they were still under indictment for the murders of Albert J. Fountain and Kent Kearney. All of the charges against Lee, Gililland, and McNew were dismissed by the end of the summer of 1899.

Records show that the investigation didn't stop there, as further attempts were made, at least by Garrett and Williams, through 1900 to investigate the case, find more witnesses, and search for the bodies. Nothing substantial developed.

No one was ever tried for the murder of Colonel Albert Jennings Fountain.[10]

nineteen

In Conclusion

Who killed Colonel Albert Jennings Fountain and Henry Fountain? In telling this story, I've attempted to lay out all of the surviving evidence.

Over the years, the more people spoke of this mystery, the more names have been added to the list of suspects. The following is a list of the men who have been mentioned as suspects or possible conspirators in this crime at one time or another: Oliver Lee, James Gililland, William McNew, Ed Brown, Green Scott, Emerald James, William Carr, Tom Tucker, Jack Tucker, Albert B. Fall, Hiram Yost, John Yost, Frank Hill, Frank Chatfield, --- Thergood, José Chavez y Chavez, Tom "Black Jack" Ketchum, Sam Ketchum, Joe Morgan, William Gililland, Print Rhodes, Charles Jones, Jim Miller, Randolph Reynolds, --- Brady, William Johnson, Fred Pellman, --- Stiles, Bob Raley, Tom Priedemore, John Lynch, Jim Lynch, --- Johnson (William?), --- Grady, Gene ---, Len Watts, Luis Herrera, and --- Lillaret.[1]

Many of these men where not mentioned as suspects until years after the murders, because at the time no evidence was found linking them to the crime, and in some cases they even had an airtight alibi. Take José Chavez y Chavez, who has been cited by many over the years as one of the men believed to have killed the Fountains. Former Sheriff and Governor George Curry put this suspect in everyone's minds when he wrote in his autobiography, many years after the disappearance, that Chavez y Chavez was among those Fountain prosecuted during the January 1896 court session in Lincoln. Curry added that he believed Chavez y Chavez was wrongly prosecuted and that he was acquitted.

Curry claimed that a day or two before Colonel Fountain left Lincoln, Chavez y Chavez called him into the saloon opposite the courthouse, inviting him to have a drink. Chavez y Chavez talked to him about the case and protested his innocence, which Curry believed.

"George," he said, "I will do anything for you and as I have promised you, I will do nothing here, but I will get that scoundrel Fountain if I have to hang for it."

Curry wrote, "I have never seen Chavez y Chavez since, but learned later that he was at Luna's wells near the White Sands the night before Colonel Fountain was killed in the 'Chalk Hills' a few miles away."

Curry added that years later he asked Ed Brown who participated in the Fountain murders.

"George," Brown replied, "I am sworn to secrecy. I know the names of all the participants but I will never tell. I will do this; if you ask me, I will tell you who was not there."

Curry asked, "Was Oliver Lee there?"

"No, Oliver Lee was too chicken hearted," Brown said.

"Was Billy McNew there?"

Brown did not answer.

"Was Jim Gililland there?"

Again no answer.

"Was Randolph Reynolds there?"

No answer.

"Was José Chavez y Chavez there?"

No answer.[2]

So, José Chavez y Chavez became a much-accused suspect. One problem was that José Chavez y Chavez was in jail at the time of the Fountain disappearance. He was awaiting trial for another murder.[3]

Other men who had no evidence found against them in the investigation from 1896 to 1900 are Tom Ketchum, Sam Ketchum, William Gililland, John Yost, Jim Miller, Randolph Reynolds, Print Rhodes, Fred Pellman, any man named Brady, Stiles, Cleavers, or Grady, Bob Raley, Tom Priedemore, John Lynch, or Jim Lynch. The only information against any of these men was some old-timer's story told many years after the fact.

Luis Herrera, Lillaret, and Len Watts were all mentioned to Garrett in letters, the information in each case coming from someone who heard it from someone else who heard it from someone else. Further investigation into these men led to nothing.

Johnson's only connection was that he told Governor Otero that he was at Sunol at the time of the murder and said that he could locate the bodies. No record exists of him being a suspect or being near Chalk Hill at the time of the murder.

Hiram Yost, Frank Hill, and Charles Jones had been at Fall's Sunol property as late as January 30, 1896. Nothing links them to the murders, nor was there physical evidence that the killers came from Sunol.

That leaves us with the most likely participants. Was it a party led by Ed Brown and possibly including Green Scott, Emerald James, Thergood, a man named Gene, or an unknown Mexican; or did the party who murdered the Fountains consist of a combination of either Oliver Lee, James Gililland, William McNew, Tom Tucker, Jack Tucker, William Carr, Joe Morgan, Frank Chatfield, and with possibly Albert Fall as the mastermind behind it?

Was it Ed Brown's group? José Angel Gallegos said that Ed Brown, Green Scott, and another man left Brown's ranch in the latter part of January and returned a few days after Fountain's disappearance with very worn out horses. Alexander Garcia made the same statement, and added that the men acted in a very suspicious manner after their return. Bursum said that he was told that Brown came into San Marcial a few days after Fountain was killed with his horse in very bad shape. William Steen stated that on February 3, 1896, Brown and Emerald James rode into the corral of S. J. Hanna. Their horses were worn out and both lay down as soon as the saddles were removed. Hanna confirmed this. Steen also said that the heels of both of Brown's boots were gone. Steen did not notice firearms on Brown or James. Brown's alibi was suspect and no one could agree upon the exact dates. Brown told everyone who would listen that he could find the bodies and did not seem worried about being implicated in the case. Elfego Baca said he spoke to Green Scott about the killing once, and Scott told him, "that he was glad of it and wished to God they had gotten the rest of the family." The only mention of Thergood had him with Brown and James about five days before the murder. Pinkerton operative Sayers was unable to get information linking Brown with the crime nor any information from him. The trails the search party found went the direction opposite of San Marcial, where Brown was seen on the third of February. If he was involved, he headed east (to dispose of the bodies?) before heading home. The information against Brown was all based on suspicious activity following the murders, with no actual evidence linking him to the crime.

Were Oliver Lee, James Gililland, Bill McNew, Jack Tucker, Tom Tucker, William Carr, Joe Morgan, and Frank Chatfield among the men who held up the Fountains at Chalk Hill? Was Albert Fall behind it all? First, we can eliminate Frank Chatfield from this group. His name turned up in the statement of Eva Taylor and no place else. Lee and McNew were seen together before and after the murder. There was never the mention of a Chatfield with them or anywhere else in the vicinity. Even Taylor said of the man with Lee and McNew, "The third man I think was Frank Chatfield, but am not certain." Could this Frank Chatfield look similar to James Gililland? Jack Tucker and William Carr were seen watching

Fountain by José Hermosillo and another man. Adam Dieter saw Carr and Tucker watching Fountain in Tularosa. More second-hand information said that others saw Carr and Tucker watching Fountain. Judge Bailey saw Tucker watching Fountain in Tularosa. There was no mention of Tom Tucker or Joe Morgan's presence during any of this. Witnesses state that Morgan was at Fall's Sunol ranch around the time of the murder. The tracks of the three horse-men who held up the Fountains at Chalk Hill appeared to lead di-rectly to Oliver Lee's Dog Canyon and Wildy Well ranches, at least by most of the searching party. There is no question that the trails at the very least went in the general direction of these ranches. The evidence of Lee's horse matching a set of horse tracks the search party followed, and of McNew's boot matching tracks they saw at the campsite was well laid out in the trial of Lee and Gililland and at McNew's preliminary hearing.

As for Albert Fall, his alibi holds up. Fall was not at Chalk Hill when the Fountains were killed. Was he the mastermind behind the entire affair? One can only speculate. There was no evidence to show that he was. Still, because of his close relationship with some of the suspects, it is possible.

All that being said, it was no surprise that Lee and Gililland were acquitted. The prosecution had problems from the start, including missing witnesses and Jack Maxwell's faulty memory. They failed to call Eva Taylor, presumably for character reasons, even though she was an eyewitness to Lee, McNew, and a third man she could not identify. To be frank, the defense outperformed the prosecution.

There was ample evidence collected against Oliver Lee and Bill McNew. James Gililland was a different story, however. There was very little evidence presented at the trial, or even gathered at that time, which linked him with the crime. Was Gililland the third man? Over the years, there had been little talking from people close to the case, but there had been some. Lucy Raley, Jim Gililland's sister, was one. In 1915, her husband was killed by Bill McNew and she was wounded by a bullet to the neck. Mrs. Raley afterwards wrote a letter to Albert Fountain. "I write this in great fear. One of the men who killed your father and little brother has just killed my husband. If I had done my duty on the stand (although it would have ruined my brother), it is possible my husband would still be alive."[4]

Lucy Raley supposedly told another story, probably the story she regretted not sharing on the stand. She said that when she was a young girl working at Lee's Dog Canyon ranch, she saw one or more of the three suspects digging up the remains of Henry Fountain from a shallow grave. The nearby hogs tore at the boy.[5]

It's possible the guilt of killing a child stayed with Gililland his entire life, driving him to drink and talk. There were various rumors that he did talk. One such story was told by Butler Oral "Snooks" Burris. Now it should be noted that according to the family of Gililland, Burris was "known by the New Mexico mountain folks to be typically in his cups and totally untrustworthy."[6] Leon Metz, Pat Garrett's biographer, who interviewed Burris in 1969, does not dispute this possibility.[7] Judging by their actions, the Fountain family put at least some credence in the story, and still do.[8]

Burris knew James Gililland for the last decade of Gililland's life. Over time, Burris would come to call him "Uncle Jim." The two met when Burris, with his father, wanted to purchase Gililland's ranch in 1937. After the selling price had been negotiated, Burris agreed to wait sixty days to take possession. During that time, he and Gililland spent much time together, talking and drinking. Burris said that as Gililland had gotten to know him better, Gililland began calling attention to a grave in the San Andreas. The grave was marked by a pillar of stone. "Son, that grave holds a lot of secrets," Gililland would say. Burris didn't ask questions. Over time, Gililland began to talk about the Fountains, the necessity for getting rid of the colonel, and how no one knew what exactly had happened. "Rumor has them buried on my ranch," he would say with a wink. Gililland eventually pointed out the grave. He said that the Fountains were buried there twenty years before, after being moved from another spot. He only recently marked the grave. Burris claimed that Gililland talked about the murders a lot. The killing of the colonel did not bother Gililland, but the killing of Henry did. He told Burris how it had happened. He said that Lee, McNew, and himself had pulled alongside the Fountains and began shooting as Fountain frantically lashed his horses in a futile attempt to escape. As many shots had been fired, they did not know who hit the colonel. "Har, har, har!" Gililland laughed, "that old son of a bitch jumped out of that wagon like a big toad. He hopped directly between the two horse riggings, and was dead when we reached him." Then came Henry's death. Gililland would pour whisky down when he told it. The boy, Gililland said, was killed because "dead men tell no tales." At the camp, Lee, McNew, and himself drew straws, Gililland getting the short one. Without a word, he pulled out his knife, opened it, grabbed Henry by his hair, pulled his head back, and "cut the little feller's throat." His body was thrown into a pit of alkaline.

At a later date, when Gililland lived at Hot Springs, he handed Burris a Masonic Pin. He said he took it off the Colonel's body, and asked Burris to give it to Albert Fountain when he was gone. Following Gililland's death, the pin was given to the Fountain family, who pronounced it authentic. In 1950, a party went to the marker in the San Andreas. They dug, but found no bodies, not even evidence that the earth there had ever been disturbed.[9]

Does the lack of remains mean Burris lied, or had Gililland marked the wrong spot after so many years? Burris's story closely fits the evidence found, with the exception of how they overtook Fountain's buggy, as no one was mentioned to have been off of his horse and behind a bush. But Burris told the story years after he had heard it from a man telling it forty years after the fact. Another problem is if Gililland slit Henry's throat at the campsite, why was no blood found there? The search party covered that ground pretty well. Was it covered in sleet like the first pool of blood?

The question remains, what happened to the Fountain bodies? One story said they were cremated in the firebox of one of Oliver Lee's steam pumps.[10]

In 1900, two charred skeletons were found in James Canyon in the Sacramento Mountains, five miles from Cloudcroft. Garrett said they were not the remains of the Fountains. Jack Fountain, it was said, was not so sure.[11]

It was 1909 when the Masonic Lodge in Las Cruces received a letter with a Texas postmark asking if the reward for finding the bodies was still outstanding. Historian C. L. Sonnichsen wrote that "the signature on the bottom of the page was a familiar one in the Tularosa country." The Masons said that the reward was available. A letter then came directing the searchers to an area north of the Jarillas. A search party was organized and Albert Fountain was sent for. The men were ready to go when Albert Fountain, "in a terrible state," was asked if he was going with them.

"My God no," Fountain exclaimed, "it would kill my mother." The search was called off and the Masons withdrew their reward.[12]

The location of the Fountain bodies remains a mystery.

What I Believe Happened To The Fountains

When Albert J. and Henry Fountain left Blazer's Mill on the morning of January 31, they were not alone. Shadowing them from a distance were Jack Tucker and William Carr. The two men followed the Fountains the entire day. That night, as Albert and Henry slept in La Luz, Carr and Tucker rode down to Lee's Dog Canyon ranch to notify the men waiting there where the Fountains were. That's when Oliver Lee, William McNew, and James Gililland picked up the trail. They trailed the pair, got ahead, and near Chalk Hill ambushed the father and son. One of the men was on foot behind a bush. The other two charged out on horseback. Albert Fountain was shot before he could do anything to protect himself or his son. Frightened by the gunshots, the horses turned off the road. As the buckboard turned, Fountain fell out of the buckboard, dead or close to it already. The men on horseback chased the buckboard as the third man probably walked over to check on Fountain. When the buckboard was brought back, Fountain's dead body was thrown over one of his horses. The lack of blood in the buckboard suggests that Henry survived the initial shooting, but the bloodstained nickel and dime found indicate he may have been killed before they left the roadside. No second pool of blood was found there or anywhere else for that matter. Whether it was at the roadside, the camp, or somewhere else, there is no doubt that the men who killed the colonel killed Henry too. They had to, for the simple reason that dead men tell no tales.

Oliver Lee's Dog Canyon ranch house, 1943.
(Photographer unknown. Courtesy of University of Texas at El Paso Library, Special Collections Department, C. L. Sonnichsen papers, No. 141-62-74-559.)

Grave of James Gililland and his wife Adella. Tularosa Fairview
Cemetery.
(Author's photograph, 2004.)

Wildy Well ruins, 2006.
(Author's photograph.)

Mesilla, the plaza, 2004.
(Author's photograph.)

Colonel Fountain's Mesilla home, 2004.
(Author's photograph.)

Epilogues

New Mexico finally became a state in 1912. It was the forty-seventh state admitted to the Union.

William McNew spent his life as a rancher. In 1915 he shot and killed Bob Raley, James Gililland's brother-in-law. McNew died on the thirtieth day of June, 1937.[1]

James Gililland started a ranch in 1902 and stayed there almost forty years. Upon selling the ranch, he and his wife spent a year traveling the eastern states. They settled in Hot Springs (now Truth or Consequences), New Mexico, where Jim Gililland died on August 8, 1946.[2]

Albert Bacon Fall went on to serve various government posts in New Mexico, but he longed to serve at the national level. As New Mexico got closer to statehood, Fall separated himself from the Democratic Party and then switched to the Republican Party. Although other reasons contributed, a driving force was surely the knowledge that once statehood was achieved, the senators elected from this heavily Republican state would be Republicans. The switch paid off. In 1912, Albert Fall and Thomas Catron became the first two senators elected from the state of New Mexico.

Fall served on the Senate until 1921, when he resigned to accept an appointment by President Warren G. Harding to the position of secretary of the interior. Fall resigned that office in 1923, as the principal figure in the scandal that became known as Teapot Dome.

He was tried, found guilty of conspiracy to defraud the government of the United States, and spent one year in the New Mexico Penitentiary, becoming the first cabinet member ever imprisoned for a crime committed while in office. His health slowly deteriorated from the early 1920s on. Fall died in 1944.[3]

Oliver Lee kept busy with ranching and politics over the next forty years and became a very prominent cattleman. Lee, like Fall, switched to the Republican Party. He served as the Republican county chairman and between 1918 and 1932 he split time between the State Legislature and Senate. While in the legislature and senate, it was said that Lee always kept a loaded .45 under his coat, a claim his family denies. Oliver Lee died on December 15, 1941, in Alamogordo.[4]

William H. H. Llewellyn was appointed to the office of United States District Attorney in 1901 by his friend, President Theodore Roosevelt. Llewellyn fought vigorously for New Mexico's statehood, took part in the constitutional convention in 1910, and in 1911 became a member of New Mexico's first legislature after it became a state. Llewellyn died on June 11, 1927.[5]

Grave of William H. H. Llewellyn, Masonic Cemetery, Las Cruces, 2004.
(Author's photograph.)

Thomas Branigan spent 1899 and 1900 as the Doña Ana County Assessor, spent eight years as a member and treasurer of the Doña Ana Republican Central Committee, spent time on the Las Cruces school board, and did other public works. Branigan died in 1925.[6]

John Conklin Fraser moved up and up in the Pinkerton National Detective Agency. He moved west to San Francisco in 1906 and became manager of the Pacific Division. He spent much time in San Francisco and Los Angeles before finally settling in Los Angeles. Following his retirement in 1933, Robert Pinkerton wrote of Fraser:

> Mr. Fraser came to the agency in 1880 at the age of twenty, and throughout these many years, his efforts have been diligent and eminently successful. As operative, Assistant Superintendent, Superintendent and Division Manager, he has shown unusual devotion and loyalty to the Agency and to my family. Having worked under and known personally each generation of Pinkertons, from the founder to myself [four generations], he has had the respect and friendship of us all.

Fraser, whose first marriage had ended in divorce, left early the next year on a tour of the world with his second wife, Adeline. John Fraser died on July 25, 1938.[7]

Pat Garrett did not seek re-election at the end of his term as sheriff.

In 1901, President Roosevelt appointed Garrett Collector of Customs at El Paso. Unfortunately, a small scandal centering on questions of Garrett's character caused him to not be re-appointed. So, in 1906, Garrett moved his family back to New Mexico. Some say he returned to find the Fountain bodies. Whatever the reason

John C. Fraser
(Date and photograph
unknown. Courtesy
of the Library of
Congress, Pinkerton
National Detective
Agency collection.)

for his return, he spent his remaining days ranching, gambling, moody, and broke.

Garrett became involved in a fight over the use of land that he was leasing to others. The battle ended for Garrett on February 29, 1908, with a bullet to the back of his head while urinating. A man named Wayne Brazel confessed to the shooting and claimed self-defense. He was defended by Albert B. Fall and acquitted. Despite the confession, there is debate among historians over who actually pulled the trigger.

Pat Garrett was an agnostic. At his funeral, his favorite page from the Great Agnostic's works was read:

> Life is a narrow vale between the cold and
> barren peaks of two eternities. We strive in vain to
> look beyond the heights. We cry aloud—and the
> only answer is the echo of our wailing cry. From the

voiceless lips of the unreplying dead there comes no word. But in the night of death Hope sees a star and listening love can hear the rustling of a wing.[8]

Garrett family plot. Pat's marker is on the left. Masonic Cemetery, Las Cruces, 2002.
(Author's photograph.)

NOTES

Abbreviations:

CSWR-UNM: Center for Southwest Research,
University of New Mexico.

MSSU: Missouri Southern State University.

NARA: National Archives and Records Administration.

RGHC-NMSU: Rio Grande Historical Collections,
New Mexico State University.

SSCD-UTEP: Sonnichsen Special Collections Department,
University of Texas at El Paso.

NMSRCA: New Mexico State Records Center and Archives.

Notes to Chapter One

[1] Owen, *The Two Alberts: Fountain and Fall*, 9; *The Handbook of Texas Online*, s.v. "Fountain, Albert Jennings."

[2] Gibson, *The Life and Death of Colonel Albert Jennings Fountain*, 5.

[3] Sonnichsen, *Tularosa: Last of the Frontier West*, 56.

[4] Gibson, *Life and Death*, 6; Sonnichsen, *Tularosa*, 56; Katie Stoes notes, Ms 208, Katie Stoes collection, RGHC-NMSU.

[5] Owen, *The Two Alberts*, 11–12; *The Handbook of Texas Online*, s.v. "Fountain, Albert Jennings."

[6] Gibson, *Life and Death*, 8–9; Service Record of Albert J. Fountain, 1861–66, NARA.

[7] Service Record of Albert J. Fountain.

[8] Gibson, *Life and Death*, 10–20; *The Handbook of Texas Online*, s.v. "Fountain, Albert Jennings."

[9] Owen, *The Two Alberts*, 21; *The Handbook of Texas Online*, s.v. "Fountain, Albert Jennings."

[10] Service Record of Albert J. Fountain.

[11] *History of New Mexico: Its Resources and People: Illustrated*: Volume I, 349–50.

[12] Gibson, *Life and Death*, 39–43; *Rio Grande Republican*, Jan. 16, 1891; Service Records of Albert J. Fountain, NARA.

[13] Gibson, *Life and Death*, 42.

[14] Gibson, *Life and Death*, 43–44; *Rio Grande Republican*, Jan. 16, 1891.

[15] Gibson, *Life and Death*, 43–45, 48, 50; Owen, *The Two Alberts*, 37–38; *By-Laws of Aztec Lodge, No. 3*, 28; *The Handbook of Texas Online*, s.v. "Fountain, Albert Jennings."

[16] Konstam, *The Civil War: A Visual Encyclopedia*, 372–73.

[17] Gibson, *Life and Death*, 54–56; *The Handbook of Texas Online*, s.v. "Fountain, Albert Jennings."

[18] Gibson, *Life and Death*, 64, 66, 74 and 83; Sonnichsen, *Tularosa*, 59.

[19] Owen, *The Two Alberts*, 69.

[20] Gibson, *Life and Death*, 77–79; Owen, *The Two Alberts*, 69–72; *Austin State Journal*, December 22, 1870.

[21] Owen, *The Two Alberts*, 79–81.

[22] *By-Laws of Aztec Lodge, No. 3*, 20–21, 24–25, 27–28, 30–32, 37.

[23] Gibson, *Life and Death*, 93–93 and 96–97.

[24] Keleher, *Violence in Lincoln County*, 320–21; Nolan, *The Lincoln County War: A Documentary History*, 414.

[25] Owen, *The Two Alberts*, 100.

[26] Gibson, *Life and Death*; *The Handbook of Texas Online*, s.v. "Fountain, Albert Jennings."

[27] Nolan, *The Lincoln County War*, 47; Owen, *The Two Alberts*, 151–52; Utley, *High Noon in Lincoln: Violence on the Western Frontier*, 24–25.

Notes to Chapter Two

[1] *Rio Grande Republican*, November 12, 1888; *Santa Fe New Mexican*, November 10, 1888.

[2] Gibson, *Life and Death of Colonel Albert Jennings Fountain*; Owen, *The Two Alberts: Fountain and Fall*, 167, 171; *Rio Grande Republican*, November 12, 1888; *Santa Fe New Mexican*, November 10, 1888.

[3] Biographical Directory of the United States Congress: Fall, Albert Bacon.

[4] Owen, *The Two Alberts*, 239; Sonnichsen, *Tularosa: Last of the Frontier West*, 70.

[5] Service Record of Albert B. Fall, National Archives.

[6] Gibson, *The Life and Death of Colonel Albert Jennings Fountain*, 192; Metz, *Pat Garrett: The Story of a Western Lawman*, 167; Owen, *The Two Alberts*; Sonnichsen, *Tularosa*, 69.

[7] Notes in Weisner Papers, Box 37, Folder F 4, RGHC-NMSU.

[8] *Rio Grande Republican*, November 13, 1890.

[9] Keleher, *The Fabulous Frontier: Twelve New Mexico Items*, 186–87; Metz, *Pat Garrett*, 168; Sonnichsen, *Tularosa*, 76–77.

[10] Bloom and Walter, *New Mexico Historical Review* 2, p. 306; Bloom and Walter, *New Mexico Historical Review* 14, p. 12; The Spanish American War Centennial Website, www.spanamwar.com/rrmllewellyn.htm.

[11] *History of New Mexico: Its Resources and People: Illustrated*: Volume II, 569; www.hipnt.com, Time Line for Thomas Branigan and Thomas Branigan Home Page.

[12] Owen, *The Two Alberts*, 265, 268.

[13] Gibson, *The Life and Death of Colonel Albert Jennings*

Fountain, 219–20; Sonnichsen, *Tularosa: Last of the Frontier West,* 90; Southeastern New Mexico Stock Growers' Association Contract with Albert J. Fountain, March 20, 1894, Gibson Collection, MSSU.

¹⁴ Gibson, *Life and Death*, 221; Sonnichsen, *Tularosa*, 95–96.

¹⁵ Gibson, *Life and Death*, 222; Records of convicts, New Mexico Penitentiary, Ely E. Miller, NMSRCA.

¹⁶ Ibid., 222–23; *Rio Grande Republican*, December 1, 1894.

¹⁷ Read, *Illustrated History of New Mexico*, 658.

¹⁸ *Rio Grande Republican*, March 29, 1895.

¹⁹ Gibson, *Life and Death*, 204–9; Metz, *Pat Garrett: The Story of a Western Lawman*, 177–78; Owen, *The Two Alberts: Fountain and Fall*, 270.

²⁰ Owen, *The Two Alberts*, 272, 277, 302.

²¹ Sonnichsen, *Tularosa*, 30–31; ancestry.com; Pinkerton Reports; 1940 Federal Census listing of Oliver M. Lee in Alamogordo, N.M.

²² Sonnichsen, *Tularosa*, 31.

²³ Sonnichsen, *Tularosa*, 81–82; alvyray.com: The Fountain Murders; Author's correspondence with Alvy Ray Smith, 2003.

²⁴ McNew and McNew, *Pioneers of 1885 in New Mexico*, 221.

²⁵ Sonnichsen, *Tularosa*, 81.

²⁶ Katie Stoes notes, box 139, folder 1125, Sonnichsen collection, SSCD-UTEP.

²⁷ Gibson, *Life and Death*, 229.

²⁸ Letter from Fountain to Cree, October 3, 1895, RGHC-NMSU.

²⁹ Gibson, *Life and Death*, 211; Sonnichsen, *Tularosa*, 108.

³⁰ Letter from Fountain to Cree, October 3, 1895.

³¹ Gibson, *Life and Death*, 226; *Rio Grande Republican*, November 15, 1895.

Notes to Chapter Three

[1] Gibson, *The Life and Death of Colonel Albert Jennings Fountain*, 227; Metz, *Pat Garrett: The Story of a Western Lawman*, 170; O'Connor, *Pat Garrett*, 190; Owen, *The Two Alberts: Fountain and Fall*, 283–84; Sonnichsen, *Tularosa: Last of the Frontier West*, 115–16.

[2] Gibson, *Life and Death*, 228; *El Paso Herald*, May 31, 1899.

[3] Keleher, *The Fabulous Frontier: Twelve New Mexico Items*, 207; Lincoln Court Records, January 21, 1896, Weisner Papers, RGHC-NMSU.

[4] Sonnichsen, *Tularosa*, 117.

[5] Keleher, *Fabulous Frontier*, 208.

[6] Collection Ms 110: Mill abstract and Joseph Hoy Blazer Biographical sketch, Blazer Family Papers, 1864–1965, RGHC-NMSU.

[7] *El Paso Times*, April 16, 1898.

[8] Sonnichsen, *Tularosa*, 118.

[9] Gibson, *Life and Death*, 230–31; *El Paso Herald*, June 2, 3, 1899; *El Paso Times*, April 12, 1898; Pinkerton Reports, March 6, 1896.

[10] Pinkerton reports, March 6, 1896; *El Paso Herald*, February 4, 1896; Author's observations of Chalk Hill.

[11] Gibson, *Life and Death*, 232–33; Sonnichsen, *Tularosa: Last of the Frontier West*, 124; Katie Stoes Notes, box 139, folder 1125, Sonnichsen Collection, SSCD-UTEP; Weisner papers, box 29, ms 249, folder 7, RGHC-NMSU; Witness list for the defense, New Mexico Archives; *El Paso Herald*, May 31, June 1, 2, and 6, 1899.

[12] *El Paso Herald*, May 31, 1899, June 1, 5, 1899; *Socorro Chieftain*, February 14, 1896; Pinkerton Reports, March 7, 1896.

[13] Sonnichsen, *Tularosa*, 125; *El Paso Herald*, February 14, 1896, and May 31, June 1, and June 5, 1899.

[14] Pinkerton Reports, March 15, 1896.

[15] Gibson, *Life and Death*, 234–35.

[16] Sonnichsen, *Tularosa*, 126; *El Paso Herald*, May 3, 31, 1899.

[17] *El Paso Herald*, June 1, 3, 5, and 6, 1899; *Rio Grande Republican*, June 9, 1899.

[18] *El Paso Times*, February 5, 1896.

[19] *Santa Fe New Mexican*, February 19, 1896.

[20] Gibson, *Life and Death*, 235–36; Sonnichsen, *Tularosa*, 128; *El Paso Herald*, May 31 and June 6, 1899; *Santa Fe New Mexican*, May 31, 1899.

[21] *El Paso Herald*, June 1, 1899; *Santa Fe New Mexican*, May 31, 1899.

[22] Fergusson, *Murder and Mystery in New Mexico*, 81; Sonnichsen, *Tularosa*, 127–28; *El Paso Herald*, June 3 and June 5, 1899; *El Paso Times*, April 12, 1898.

[23] *El Paso Herald*, June 7, 1899; *El Paso Times*, April 13, 1898.

Notes to Chapter Four

[1] *El Paso Times*, February 4, 1896.

[2] *Santa Fe New Mexican*, February 5, 1896.

[3] *Socorro Chieftain*, February 21, 1896.

[4] Pinkerton reports, March 4, 6, 1896; Gibson, *The Life and Death of Colonel Albert Jennings Fountain*, 242.

[5] Gibson, *Life and Death*, 239; Metz, *Pat Garrett: The Story of a Western Lawman*, 175.

[6] *El Paso Herald*, February 4, 1896.

[7] *Rio Grande Republican*, February 14, 1896.

[8] Owen, *The Two Alberts: Fountain and Fall*, 298–99; *Santa Fe New Mexican*, February 8 and 17, 1896; *Socorro Chieftain*, February 21, 1896.

[9] Garrett, *The Authentic Life of Billy, the Kid*, introduction by Dykes (1954 ed.), XI-XIV; Metz, *Pat Garrett*; Tuska, *Billy the Kid, His Life and Legend*, 75; Utley, *Billy the Kid: A Short and Violent Life*, 135–36; Garrett family tree, ancestry.com.

[10] Gibson, *Life and Death*, 243–44; Metz, *Pat Garrett*, 178–79;

Owen, *The Two Alberts*, 299; Sonnichsen, *Tularosa: Last of the Frontier West*, 142; *Rio Grande Republican*, February 21, 1896.

[11] *Roswell Record*, March 4, 1896.

[12] Metz, *Pat Garrett*, 179.

[13] Garrett, *Authentic Life*, introduction by Jarvis Garrett (1964 ed.), 25–26.

[14] Pinkerton reports; Garrett, *Authentic Life*, introduction by Jarvis Garrett (1964 ed.), 25–26; Metz, *Pat Garrett*, 179.

[15] Ball, "Lawman in Disgrace: Sheriff Charles C. Perry of Chaves County, New Mexico," *New Mexico Historical Review* 61, 124–36; Pinkerton reports.

[16] Garrett, *Authentic Life*, introduction by Jarvis Garrett (1964 ed.), 25.

[17] Eva Taylor's statement, undated, NMSRCA; Pinkerton reports, March 4, 8, and 10, 1896.

[18] Eva Taylor's statement, undated.

[19] Pinkerton reports, March 8, 10, 1896.

[20] Undated Document (written by Williams?), NMSRCA.

[21] Ibid., next document in archives regarding investigation into the murder of Albert J. Fountain.

[22] Ibid, first document in archives regarding investigation into the murder of Albert J. Fountain (same as footnote 8).

[23] Ibid., second document in archives (same as footnote 9).

[24] Ibid., first document in archives.

[25] Letter from P. F. Garrett to his wife, March 1, 1896, Bowlins-Fort Sumner Museum.

Notes to Chapter Five

[1] Pinkertons.com (history).

[2] Letter from James Cree to Governor Thornton, February 17, 1896; Letter from Thornton to James McParland (apparently the second letter regarding this matter) February 27, 1896; Letter from Col. Fountain to Cree, October 3, 1895, RGHC-NMSU.

[3] Letter from McParland to Thornton, February 28, 1896, RGHC-NMSU.

[4] Pinkerton reports, March 2–4, 1896.

[5] Ibid., March 4, 1896.

[6] Ibid., March 5, 1896.

[7] Ibid., March 5–April 4, 1896.

[8] Ibid., March 6, 1896.

[9] Ibid.

[10] Ibid.

[11] Ibid., March 7, 1896.

[12] Sonnichsen, *Tularosa: Last of the Frontier West*, 128–29.

[13] Bloom and Walter, *New Mexico Historical Review* 1, 490; Pinkerton reports, March 7, 1896.

[14] Pinkerton reports, March 7, 1896.

[15] Ibid.

[16] Pinkerton reports, March 8, 1896.

[17] Ibid.

[18] Ibid., March 10, 1896.

[19] Letter from Thornton to Fraser, March 10, 1896, RGHC-NMSU.

[20] Pinkerton reports, March 10–11, 1896.

[21] Ibid., March 11, 1896.

[22] Ibid., March 12, 1896.

[23] Ibid., March 8 and 12, 1896.

Notes to Chapter Six

[1] Metz, *Pat Garrett: The Story of a Western Lawman*, 199; Pinkerton reports, March 13, 1896.

[2] Pinkerton reports, March 13, 1896.

[3] Ibid., March 14, 1896.

[4] Letter from Thornton to Fraser, March 13, 1896, RGHC-NMSU.

[5] Pinkerton report, March 15, 1896.

[6] Ibid.

[7] *History of New Mexico: Its Resources and People: Illustrated*: Volume I, 452–53; Pinkerton reports, March 16, 1896; 1900 Federal Census for New San Marcial, New Mexico.

[8] Owen, *The Two Alberts: Fountain and Fall*, 272; Pinkerton reports, March 17, 1896.

[9] Pinkerton reports, March 17, 1896.

[10] Ibid., March 16, 1896.

[11] Ibid.

[12] Ibid.

[13] Ibid., March 17, 1896.

[14] Keleher, *The Fabulous Frontier: Twelve New Mexico Items*, 94; *The Handbook of Texas Online*, s.v. "Sutton-Taylor Feud."

[15] Pinkerton reports, March 18, 1896.

[16] Ibid.

[17] Ibid.

[18] Sonnichsen, *Tularosa: Last of the Frontier West*, 140.

[19] Pinkerton reports, March 18, 1896.

[20] Ibid., March 18 and 20, 1896.

[21] Ibid., March 18, 1896.

Notes to Chapter Seven

[1] Pinkerton reports, March 19, 1896.

[2] Ibid.

[3] Ibid., March 20, 1896.

[4] Ibid.

[5] Metz, *Pat Garrett: The Story of a Western Lawman*, 200.

[6] Pinkerton reports, March 21, 1896.

[7] Ibid., March 22, 1896.

[8] Ibid.

[9] Ibid.

[10] Ibid.

[11] Ibid., March 23, 1896.

[12] Ibid., March 24, 1896.

Notes to Chapter Eight

[1] Pinkerton reports, March 24, 1896; Letter from McParland to Thornton, February 28, 1896, RGHC-NMSU.

[2] Pinkerton reports, March 25, 1896.

[3] Ibid., March 6, 1896.

[4] Ibid., March 25, 1896.

[5] Ibid.

[6] Ibid., March 26, 1896.

[7] *El Paso Herald*, June 3, 1899.

[8] Letter from Thornton to Fraser, April 4, 1896 (with Pinkerton reports), Katie Stoes collection, Ms 208, RGHC-NMSU.

[9] Letter from Fraser to Thornton, April 4, 1896 (with Pinkerton reports) Katie Stoes collection, Ms 208, RGHC-NMSU.

[10] Letter from Fraser to Thornton, April 6, 1896 (with Pinkerton reports) Katie Stoes collection, Ms 208, RGHC-NMSU.

[11] Letter From Thornton to McParland, April 7, 1896 (with Pinkerton reports) Katie Stoes collection, Ms 208, RGHC-NMSU.

[12] Letter from Fraser to Thornton, April 11, 1896 (with Pinkerton reports) Katie Stoes collection, Ms 208, RGHC-NMSU.

Notes to Chapter Nine

[1] Pinkerton reports, April 15, 1896; Pinkerton National Detective Agency Business Card, December 21, 1900, Pinkerton National Detective Agency administrative file, Box 22, Folder 4.

[2] Pinkerton reports, April 15, 1896.

[3] Gibson, *The Life and Death of Colonel Albert Jennings Fountain*, 285; Pinkerton reports, April 15, 1896.

[4] Pinkerton reports, April 16, 1896. Records of convicts, New Mexico Penitentiary, Ely E. Miller; ancestry.com, Krauss family.

[5] Pinkerton reports, April 16, 1896.

⁶ Pinkerton reports, April 17, 1896; Federal Census, Socorro, New Mexico.

⁷ Owen, *The Two Alberts: Fountain and Fall*, 276.

⁸ Pinkerton reports, April 17, 1896.

⁹ Sonnichsen, *Tularosa: Last of the Frontier West*, 98–99, 104–5.

¹⁰ Pinkerton reports, April 17, 1896.

¹¹ Sonnichsen, *Tularosa*, 45, 50–51.

¹² Pinkerton reports, April 17, 1896.

Notes to Chapter Ten

¹ Pinkerton reports, April 18, 1896.

² Pinkerton reports, April 19, 1896; Wikipedia.com: Holm O. Bursum.

³ Pinkerton reports, April 19, 1896.

⁴ Ibid., April 20, 1896.

⁵ Affidavit of William Steen, April 20, 1896 (with Pinkerton reports) Katie Stoes collection, Ms 208, RGHC-NMSU.

⁶ Pinkerton reports, April 21, 1896.

⁷ *History of New Mexico: Its Resources and People: Illustrated*: Volume II, 621; Pinkerton reports, April 22, 1896.

⁸ Pinkerton reports, April 22, 1896.

⁹ Ibid., April 23, 1896.

¹⁰ Ibid., April 24, 1896.

¹¹ Ibid., April 25, 1896.

¹² Ibid., April 26, 1896.

¹³ Pinkerton reports, May 2, 1896.

¹⁴ Ibid., May 3, 1896.

¹⁵ Ibid., May 4, 1896.

¹⁶ Ibid., May 6, 1896.

¹⁷ Ibid., May 7, 1896.

¹⁸ Ibid., May 12, 1896.

¹⁹ Ibid., May 14, 1896.

²⁰ *Las Vegas Optic*, May 16, 1896.

Notes to Chapter Eleven

[1] Letter from C. C. Perry to P. F. Garrett, April 8, 1896; Letter from J. F. Bennett to P. F. Garrett, June 13, 1896, Folder 2, Ms 282, Pat Garrett Family Papers, RGHC-NMSU.

[2] Owen, *The Two Alberts: Fountain and Fall*, 308.

[3] Gibson, *The Life and Death of Colonel Albert Jennings Fountain*, 261; Metz, *Pat Garrett: The Story of a Western Lawman*, 200.

[4] Otero, *My Life On The Frontier, 1882–1897: Death Knell of a Territory and Birth of a State*, Volume 2, 278, 280; The Spanish American War Centennial Website, www.spanamwar.com/rrmllewellyn.htm.

[5] alvyray.com, Family database, Person Page 2 (obituary).

[6] www.hipnt.com, Time Line For Thomas Branigan and Thomas Branigan Home Page.

[7] Sonnichsen, *Tularosa: Last of the Frontier West*, 149, 151; *Rio Grande Republican*, October 9, 1896.

[8] Owen, *The Two Alberts*, 308-309.

[9] Otero, *My Nine Years as Governor of the Territory of New Mexico, 1897–1906*; Owen, *The Two Alberts*, 308–9.

[10] Gibson, *Life and Death*, 262; Owen, *The Two Alberts*, 308; Rickards, Colin, *Sheriff Pat Garrett's Last Days: The Story of the Man Who Killed Billy the Kid*, 21.

[11] *El Paso Herald*, June 7, 1899.

[12] Metz, *Pat Garrett*, 201–2.

[13] Curry, *George Curry, 1861–1947, An Autobiography*, 106; Keleher, *The Fabulous Frontier: Twelve New Mexico Items*, 218; Sonnichsen, *Tularosa*, 154.

[14] Sonnichsen, *Tularosa*, 154.

[15] Ibid.

[16] Keleher, *The Fabulous Frontier: Twelve New Mexico Items*, 2119; Sonnichsen, *Tularosa*, 154–55.

[17] Keleher, *The Fabulous Frontier*, 217.

[18] Metz, *Pat Garrett: The Story of a Western Lawman*, 203;

Sonnichsen, *Tularosa: Last of the Frontier West*, 155.

[19] *El Paso Times*, April 12, 1898.

[20] Keleher, *The Fabulous Frontier: Twelve New Mexico Items,* 219.

[21] Sonnichsen, *Tularosa*, 157; *El Paso Times*, April 10, 1898.

[22] *Silver City Independent*, April 12, 1898.

[23] Bloom and Walter, *New Mexico Historical Review* 8, p. 377; *Rio Grande Republican*, April 15, 1898.

[24] *El Paso Herald*, June 2, 1899; *El Paso Times*, April 10, 1898; *Rio Grande Republican*, April 15, 1898.

[25] *Silver City Independent*, April 12, 1898.

[26] *El Paso Times*, April 12, 1898.

[27] Ibid., April 13, 1898.

[28] Ibid.

[29] *El Paso Times*, April 14, 1898; *Rio Grande Republican*, April 15, 1898.

[30] *El Paso Times*, April 15, 16, 1896.

[31] Ibid., April 16, 1898.

[32] Ibid.

[33] Sonnichsen, *Tularosa*, 158-159; *El Paso Times*, April 16, 1898.

[34] *Rio Grande Republican*, April 15, 1898.

[35] Gibson, *The Life and Death of Colonel Albert Jennings Fountain*, 266.

Notes to Chapter Twelve

[1] Sonnichsen, *Tularosa: Last of the Frontier West*, 168.

[2] Letter to Governor Otero, July 16th, 1898, MSS 21 BC, Box 1, Miguel Otero Papers, CSWR-UNM.

[3] Bloom and Walter, *New Mexico Historical Review*: Volume 2, 306; The Spanish American War Centennial Website, www.spanam-war.com/rrmllewellyn.htm.

[4] Sheriff's criminal fee docket, Doña Ana County, 1898, Weisner Papers, RGHC-NMSU.

[5] Keleher, *The Fabulous Frontier: Twelve New Mexico Items*, 220; Metz, *Pat Garrett: The Story of a Western Lawman*, 207.

[6] Fergusson, *Murder and Mystery In New Mexico*, 86; Keleher, *Fabulous Frontier*, 220–22; Metz, *Pat Garrett*, 207–10; Sonnichsen, *Tularosa*, 160–62; *El Paso Herald*, June 7, 1899; *El Paso Times*, July 18, 1898; *Rio Grande Republican*, July 15, 1898.

[7] Keleher, *The Fabulous Frontier*, 221; *El Paso Times*, July 18, 1898.

[8] Keleher, *Fabulous Frontier*, 221; *El Paso Herald*, June 7, 1899; *El Paso Times*, July 18, 1898.

[9] Keleher, *Fabulous Frontier*, 221.

[10] *El Paso Herald*, June 7, 1899.

[11] Metz, *Pat Garrett*, 210–11; Sonnichsen, *Tularosa*, 163–64; *El Paso Herald*, June 7, 1899.

[12] Gibson, *The Life and Death of Colonel Albert Jennings Fountain*, 268.

[13] *El Paso Times*, August 29, 1898.

[14] Sonnichsen, *Tularosa: Last of the Frontier West*, 169–71.

[15] Service record of Albert B. Fall, National Archives.

[16] Otero, *My Nine Years as Governor of the Territory of New Mexico, 1897–1906*, 92; Territorial Prison at Yuma, Arizona, record for Wm. Johnson, New Mexico State Records Center; Biographical Directory of the United States Congress, Murphy, Nathan Oakes.

[17] Otero, *My Nine Years as Governor of the Territory of New Mexico, 1897–1906*, 92–93.

[18] Gibson, *Life and Death*, 270; Owen, *The Two Alberts: Fountain and Fall*, 319.

[19] Hutchinson, *Another Verdict For Oliver Lee*, 3; Metz, *Pat Garrett: The Story of a Western Lawman*, 216–18; O'Connor, *Pat Garrett*, 207–8; Sonnichsen, *Tularosa: Last of the Frontier West*, 172.

[20] Gibson, *The Life and Death of Colonel Albert Jennings Fountain*, 271; Metz, *Pat Garrett: The Story of a Western Lawman*,

219; Owen, *The Two Alberts: Fountain and Fall*, 320–22; *Socorro Chieftain*, April 28, 1899.

[21] Gibson, *Life and Death*, 272–73.

[22] Letter from T. J. Daily to the District Attorney, May 14, 1899, MSS 29, series 103, box 7, Thomas B. Catron papers, CSWR-UNM.

[23] Letter from Richmond Barnes to Thomas Catron, May 21, 1899, Catron papers, CSR-UNM.

Notes to Chapter Thirteen

Note: The transcripts for Lee and Gililland's trial, along with most of Hillsboro's records, were destroyed years ago. The trial was covered in detail in many newspapers. While some of the papers had pro-prosecution or pro-defense biases in editorials and paraphrased testimony, the direct testimony is consistent from paper to paper. These newspaper accounts were the main source in reconstructing the trial for this book. Spelling errors have been silently corrected, since the focus is on what the testimony was, not on how the newspaper reporters spelled it.

[1] Fergusson, *Murder and Mystery in New Mexico*, 87; Keleher, *The Fabulous Frontier: Twelve New Mexico Items*, 228–29; *El Paso Herald*, May 29, 1899.

[2] Keleher, *Fabulous Frontier*, 229–30; *Santa Fe New Mexican*, May 26, 1899.

[3] Gibson, *The Life and Death of Colonel Albert Jennings Fountain*, 273; Sonnichsen, *Tularosa: Last of the Frontier West*, 177.

[4] Fergusson, *Murder and Mystery in New Mexico*, 88.

[5] *El Paso Herald*, May 26, 1899; Grant County district court records.

[6] Fergusson, *Murder and Mystery*, 88–89; Grant County district court records regarding the murder of Albert J. Fountain and Henry Fountain, NMSRCA.

[7] *El Paso Herald*, May 26, 1899.

[8] Ibid, May 29, 1899.

[9] Gibson, *Life and Death*, 275; *El Paso Herald*, May 26, 27, 1899.

[10] *El Paso Herald*, May 27, 1899; *Santa Fe New Mexican*, May 27, 1899.

[11] *El Paso Herald*, May 31, 1899; *Rio Grande Republican*, June 2, 1899.

[12] *El Paso Herald*, May 31, 1899.

[13] *El Paso Herald*, May 31, 1899; *Santa Fe New Mexican*, May 31, 1899.

[14] *Rio Grande Republican*, June 2, 1899.

[15] *El Paso Herald*, June 1, 1899.

[16] Ibid.

[17] Ibid.

Notes to Chapter Fourteen

[1] *El Paso Herald*, June 2, 1899.

[2] Ibid.

[3] Ibid.

[4] Ibid.

[5] Ibid.

[6] Ibid.

Notes to Chapter Fifteen

[1] *El Paso Herald*, June 3, 1899; *Rio Grande Republican*, June 2, 1899.

[2] *El Paso Herald*, June 3, 1899; *Santa Fe New Mexican*, June 1, 1899.

[3] *El Paso Herald*, June 3, 1899; *Rio Grande Republican*, June 9, 1899.

[4] *El Paso Herald*, June 3, 1899.

[5] Ibid.

[6] *El Paso Herald*, June 3, 1899; *Rio Grande Republican*, June 9, 1899.

[7] *El Paso Herald*, June 3 and 7, 1899; *Rio Grande Republican*, June 2 and 9, 1899.

[8] *El Paso Herald*, June 7, 1899.

[9] Putnam, Julia, *The Handbook of Texas Online*, s.v. "Larn, John M."; Chuck Parsons note to author; *El Paso Herald*, June 7, 1899.

[10] El Paso Herald, June 7, 1899.

[11] Sonnichsen, *Tularosa: Last of the Frontier West*, 182; *El Paso Herald*, June 7, 1899.

[12] *El Paso Herald*, June 7, 1899.

Notes to Chapter Sixteen

[1] Fergusson, *Murder and Mystery in New Mexico*, 89; Keleher, *The Fabulous Frontier: Twelve New Mexico Items*, 235–36; *El Paso Herald*, June 5, 1899.

[2] *El Paso Herald*, June 5, 1899.

[3] Ibid.

[4] Ibid.

[5] Ibid., June 6, 1899.

[6] Ibid.

[7] *El Paso Times*, June 5, 1899; The Spanish American War Centennial Website, www.spanamwar.com/rrmllewellyn.htm.

[8] *El Paso Herald*, June 6, 1899; *El Paso Times*, June 5, 6, 1899.

[9] *El Paso Times*, June 6, 1899.

[10] Ibid.

[11] *San Luis Obispo Breeze*, March 2, 1900; *San Luis Obispo Tribune*, May 10 and June 1, 1899; Witness list for the prosecution, NMSRCA.

Notes to Chapter Seventeen

[1] *El Paso Times*, June 8, 1899.

[2] Ibid.

[3] Ibid.

[4] Ibid.; *The Herald* reported that Fitchett was there the same time as Branigan, but the testimony matched that of the Clausen incident.

[5] *El Paso Herald*, June 7, 1899; *Rio Grande Republican*, June 9, 1899.

[6] *Rio Grande Republican*, June 9, 1899.

[7] *El Paso Herald*, June 7, 1899; *Rio Grande Republican*, June 9, 1899.

[8] *El Paso Herald*, June 7, 1899; *Rio Grande Republican*, June 9, 1899; *Santa Fe New Mexican*, June 8, 1899.

[9] *El Paso Times*, June 8, 1899.

[10] Fergusson, *Murder and Mystery in New Mexico*, 82; *El Paso Times*, June 8, 1899.

[11] *El Paso Times*, June 8, 1899.

[12] Keleher, *The Fabulous Frontier: Twelve New Mexico Items*, 236–37; *El Paso Herald*, June 9, 1899; *El Paso Times*, June 8, 1899.

[13] *El Paso Herald*, June 12, 1899; *Santa Fe New Mexican*, June 9, 1899.

[14] *El Paso Herald*, June 12, 1899.

[15] Ibid.

[16] Ibid.

[17] *El Paso Herald*, June 12–13, 1899; *Las Cruces Democrat*, June 10, 1899.

[18] *El Paso Herald*, June 12, 1899.

[19] *El Paso Herald*, June 13, 1899.

[20] Ibid.

[21] Ibid.

[22] Ibid.

[23] Ibid.

[24] Ibid.

[25] Ibid.

[26] Ibid.

[27] Ibid.

Notes to Chapter Eighteen

[1] *El Paso Herald*, June 13, 1899.

[2] Ibid.

[3] Ibid., June 13 and 14, 1899.

[4] Ibid, June 14, 1899.

[5] Ibid., June 15, 1899.

[6] Bethune, *Race With the Wind: The Personal Life of Albert B. Fall*, 55.

[7] Keleher, *The Fabulous Frontier: Twelve New Mexico Items*, 238; Owen, *The Two Alberts: Fountain and Fall*, 337; *El Paso Herald*, June 15, 1899.

[8] *El Paso Herald*, June 16, 1899.

[9] Sonnichsen, *Tularosa: Last of the Frontier West*, 189; *El Paso Herald*, June 16, 1899; *Santa Fe New Mexican*, June 13, 1899.

[10] Owen, *The Two Alberts: Fountain and Fall*, 340; Sonnichsen, 189; Letters to and from Ben Williams regarding the Fountain case, from Sept. 21, 1899 through Nov. 19, 1900, NMSRCA.

Notes to Chapter Nineteen

[1] Curry, *George Curry, 1861–1947, An Autobiography*, 102–3; Garrett, *The Authentic Life of Billy, the Kid*, introduction by Jarvis Garrett (1964 ed.), 28; Owen, *The Two Alberts: Fountain and Fall*, 528–29; Pinkerton reports; Letter from Carl C. C. Perry to Pat Garrett, April 8, 1896; Letter from Carl Clausen to Pat Garrett, August 13, 1896; Eva Taylor's statement, undated, NMSRCA; Correspondence, MS 45 BC, box 10, folder 13, Erna Fergusson Papers, CRWS-UNM; Katie Stoes notes, box 139, folder 1125, Sonnichsen collection, SSCD-UTEP.

[2] Curry, *George Curry*, 102–3, 115–16.

[3] Rasch, "A Mention of José Chavez y Chavez,",*Corral Dust* 5, no. 4 (October 1960): 27, 30; *Las Vegas Daily Optic*, June 3, 1895 and December 11, 1896; Records of convicts, New Mexico Penitentiary: José Chavez y Chavez.

[4] Letter from Lucy Raley to Albert Fountain, October 27, 1915, Gibson Collection, MSSU.

[5] Gibson, *The Life and Death of Colonel Albert Jennings Fountain*, 286.

[6] Alvy Ray Smith email to author, December 6, 2003.

[7] Leon Metz email to author, December 20, 2003.

[8] *El Paso Times*, December 26 and 28, 1950; Conversation with Mary Alexander and Mary Bird, 2004.

[9] Metz, *Pat Garrett: The Story of a Western Lawman*, 229–31; *El Paso Times*, December 26 and 28, 1950.

[10] Gibson, *Life and Death*, 283.

[11] Sonnichsen, *Tularosa: Last of the Frontier West*, 192–93; Gibson, *Life and Death*, 283.

[12] Sonnichsen, *Tularosa*, 193.

Notes to Chapter Twenty

[1] McNew and McNew, *Pioneers of 1885 in New Mexico*, 221; Sonnichsen, *Tularosa: Last of the Frontier West*.

[2] alvyray.com, Family database, Person Page 2 (obituary).

[3] Owen, *The Two Alberts: Fountain and Fall*; Biographical Directory of the United States Congress: Fall, Albert Bacon; Electronic Library presents encyclopedia.com: Fall, Albert Bacon.

[4] Abousleman, *Who's Who in New Mexico*, Volume I, 129; Bloom and Walter, *New Mexico Historical Review*: Volume 2, 91; Keleher, *Memoirs: 1892–1969, A New Mexico Item*, 255; *Alamogordo Weekly News*, December 18, 1941; Gordon Owen note to author.

[5] Bloom and Walter, *New Mexico Historical Review*: Volume 2, 306; The Spanish American War Centennial Website, www.spanamwar.com/rrmllewellyn.htm.

[6] *History of New Mexico, Its Resources and People*, Volume II; www.hipnt.com, Time Line For Thomas Branigan and Thomas Branigan Home Page.

[7] 1920 Federal Census for Los Angeles, California; Divorce re-

cord for John C. and Laura Fraser, May 22, 1913, www.privateeye.
com; Telegram from I. W. Hamilton to Aster Rossetter, July 25,
1938, John C. Fraser's employment record, 1880–1938, Pinkerton
National Detective Agency administrative file, Library of Congress;
Forest Lawn-Glendale Memorial-Park cemetery records: John
Fraser, Adeline Fraser, and Irving Hamilton.

[8] Garrett, *The Authentic Life of Billy, the Kid*, introduction by
Dykes (1954 ed.), XIII – XIV; Metz, *Pat Garrett: The Story of a
Western Lawman*, 240–95; Sonnichsen, 242–43.

SOURCES

Abousleman, Michel D., *Who's Who in New Mexico*. Vol. 1. Albuquerque: The Abousleman Company, 1937.

Ball, Larry D., *Elfego Baca in Life and Legend*. El Paso: Texas Western Press, 1992.

Bethune, Martha Fall, *Race with the Wind: The Personal Life of Albert B. Fall*. El Paso: A Novio Book, 1989.

Bloom, Lansing B., and Paul A. F. Walter. *New Mexico Historical Review*. Vols. 1, 2, 14, 17. Albuquerque: Historical Society of New Mexico, 1926, 1927, 1939, 1942.

By-Laws of Aztec Lodge, No. 3. December 1, 1901.

Chávez, Thomas E. *An Illustrated History of New Mexico.* Albuquerque: University of New Mexico Press, 1992.

Curry, George. *George Curry, 1861–1974: An Autobiography.* Albuquerque: University of New Mexico Press, 1958.

Fergusson, Erna, *Murder and Mystery in New Mexico*. Albuquerque: Merle Armitage Editions, 1948.

Garrett, Pat F. *The Authentic Life of Billy, the Kid*. Intro. by J. C. Dykes. Norman: University of Oklahoma Press, 1954.

Garrett, Pat F. *The Authentic Life of Billy, the Kid*. Intro. by Jarvis Garrett. Albuquerque: Horn and Wallace, 1964.

Gibson, A. M. *The Life and Death of Colonel Albert Jennings Fountain*. Norman: University of Oklahoma Press, 1965.

Harkey, Dee. *Mean as Hell: The Life of a New Mexico Law Man.* 1948. Santa Fe: Ancient City Press, 1989.

History of New Mexico, Its Resources and People: Illustrated. Vols. 1, 2. Los Angeles: Pacific States Publishing Co., 1907.

Hutchinson, W. H. *Another Verdict for Oliver Lee.* Clarendon, TX: Clarendon Press, 1965.

Keleher, William A. *The Fabulous Frontier: Twelve New Mexico Items.* Santa Fe: Rydal Press, 1942.

———. *Memoirs, 1892–1969: A New Mexico Item.* Santa Fe: Rydal Press, 1969.

———. *Violence In Lincoln County.* Albuquerque: University of New Mexico Press, 1957.

Konstam, Angus. *The Civil War: A Visual Encyclopedia.* London: PRC Publishing, Ltd. 2001.

Metz, Leon C. *Pat Garrett: The Story of a Western Lawman.* Norman: University of Oklahoma Press, 1974.

McNew, George L., and Elizabeth McNew. *Pioneers of 1885 in New Mexico.* Las Cruces: Self-published, 1987.

Nolan, Frederick. *The Lincoln County War: A Documentary History.* Norman: University of Oklahoma Press, 1992.

O'Connor, Richard. *Pat Garrett.* New York: Doubleday, 1960.

Otero, Miguel Antonio. *My Life on the Frontier, 1882–1897: Death Knell of a Territory and Birth of a State.* Albuquerque: University of New Mexico Press, 1939.

———. *My Nine Years as Governor of the Territory of New Mexico, 1897–1906.* Albuquerque: University of New Mexico Press, 1940.

Owen, Gordon R. *The Two Alberts: Fountain and Fall.* Las Cruces: Yucca Tree Press, 1996.

Read, Benjamin M. *Illustrated History of New Mexico.* Chicago: Lewis Publishing Co., 1895.

Rickards, Colin. *Sheriff Pat Garrett's Last Days: The Story of the Man Who Killed Billy the Kid.* Santa Fe: Sunstone Press, 1986.

Siemers, Vesta, and Mary DeVarse, Mary. *Historic Walking Tour of Mesilla, NM.* Siemers, 1998.

Sonnichsen, C. L. *Tularosa: Last of the Frontier West.* Albuquerque: University of New Mexico Press, 1980.

Tuska, Jon. *Billy the Kid: His Life and Legend.* Albuquerque: University of New Mexico Press, 1994.

Utley, Robert M. *Billy the Kid: A Short and Violent Life.* Lincoln: University of Nebraska Press, 1989.

_____. *High Noon in Lincoln: Violence on the Western Frontier.* Albuquerque: University of New Mexico Press, 1987.

Articles

Ball, Larry D. "Lawman in Disgrace: Sheriff Charles C. Perry of Chaves County, New Mexico." *New Mexico Historical Review* 61, no. 1 (January 1986): 124–36.

Moore, Jack F. Jr. "The Mystery of the Fountains." *Wild West* (February 1998): 46–50, 82–83.

Pearson, George, Capt. Thomas Branigan, 1847–1925 & Time Line for Thomas Branigan. Capt. Thomas Branigan Homepage, 1998, www.newmexico.mackichan.com/lascruces/Branigan/default.htm.

Rasch, Philip J. "A Mention of Jose Chavez y Chavez." *Corral Dust* 5, no. 4 (October 1960): 27, 30.

Santana, David, Melissa Ann Villela, Rosalynn Torres, and Michael Telles. "Elfego Baca Lived More Than Nine Lives." www.epcc.edu/ftp/homes/monicaw/borderlands/22_elfego_baca.htm. El Paso Community College.

Newspapers

Alamogordo Weekly News
Austin State Journal
El Paso Herald
El Paso Times

Las Cruces Democrat
Las Vegas Optic
Los Angeles Herald-Express
Rio Grande Republican
Roswell Record
San Luis Obispo Breeze
San Luis Obispo Tribune
Santa Fe New Mexican
Silver City Independent
Socorro Chieftain

Unpublished Documents

Blazer Family Papers, 1864–1965. Rio Grande Historical
    Collections, New Mexico State University.
Pat F. Garrett Family Papers, 1859–1936. Rio Grande Historical
    Collections, New Mexico State University.
Arrel M. Gibson Collection. Missouri Southern State College.
Leon Metz Collection. C. L. Sonnichen Special Collections
    Department, University of Texas at El Paso.
Gordon Owen Collection. Rio Grande Historical Collections,
    New Mexico State University.
C. L. Sonnichsen Collection. C. L. Sonnichen Special Collections
    Department, University of Texas at El Paso.
Katherine D. Stoes Papers, 1939–1958. Rio Grande Historical
    Collections, New Mexico State University.
Herman B. Weisner Papers, 1957-1992. Rio Grande Historical
    Collections, New Mexico State University.
Doña Ana County Sheriffs Photograph Collection. Photograph
    Collections, University of Texas at El Paso.
Forest Lawn Memorial-Park, Glendale Records: John Conklin
    Fraser; Adeline Fraser; Irving Hamilton.
Marriage record of John C. Fraser to Laura S. Tinkley, January 1,
    1890. Colorado State Archives.

Pinkerton Reports of J. C. Fraser and W. B. Sayers, 1896.
Ms 208, Katie Stoes Collection, Rio Grande Historical
Collections, New Mexico State University, and box 93,
folder 402, Sonnichsen Collection, C. L. Sonnichen Special
Collections Department, University of Texas at El Paso.
1870 Federal Census, Doña Ana, New Mexico.
1900 Federal Census, New San Marcial, New Mexico.
1900 Federal Census, Socorro, New Mexico.
1920 Federal Census, Los Angeles, California.
1940 Federal Census, Alamogordo, New Mexico.

Websites

Alvyray.com: The Fountain Murders and Family Database.
Ancestry.com: Oliver M. Lee; Ely E. Miller (Krauss family);
Patrick Floyd Garrett (Kevin Greer, Greer and related fami-
lies); Hoy Family tree.
Encyclopedia.com: Fall, Albert Bacon. HighBeam Research, Inc.
Handbook of Texas Online, tsha.utexas.edu/handbook/online:
Fountain, Albert Jennings; Larn, John M.; Sutton-Taylor
Feud.
Library of Congress Online, Biographical Directory of the United
States Congress: Fall, Albert Bacon; Murphy, Nathan Oakes.
Pinkertons.com
Privateeye.com
The Spanish American War Centennial Website: William H. H.
Llewellyn. www.spanamwar.com/rrmllewellyn.htm.
Wikipedia.com: Holm O. Bursum. Wikimedia Foundation, Inc.

Archives and libraries

Bowlins-Fort Sumner Museum, Fort Sumner, New Mexico.
Gadsden Museum, Mesilla, New Mexico.
Library of Congress, Washington, D. C.

Lincoln State Monument, Lincoln, New Mexico.
Los Angeles Public Library, Los Angeles, California.
Missouri Southern State College.
    George A. Spiva Library
National Archives, Washington D. C.
New Mexico State Records Center and Archives, Santa Fe, New Mexico.
New Mexico State University, Las Cruces, New Mexico.
    Branson Hall Library
    Zuhl Library
Oliver Lee Memorial State Park, New Mexico.
Palace of the Governors, Santa Fe, New Mexico.
    Fray Angelico Chávez History Library
    Photo Archives
San Luis Obispo City-County Library, San Luis Obispo, California.
Santa Fe Public Library, Santa Fe, New Mexico.
Socorro Public Library, Socorro, New Mexico.
Thomas Branigan Memorial Library, Las Cruces, New Mexico.
University of California In Los Angeles.
    Charles E. Young Research Library
University of New Mexico, Albuquerque, New Mexico.
    Center for Southwest Research, Zimmerman Library.
University of Texas At El Paso. University Library

Correspondence/interviews referred to in text

Mary V. Alexander and Mary F. Bird (Fountain family); Dr. Alvy Ray Smith (Gililland family); Leon Metz; Gordon Owen; Chuck Parsons.

INDEX

Page numbers for illustrations appear in **boldface**